THE CRYSTAL GRID

Five Steps to the Fifth Dimension

RUBY NARIANANDA MAYO
and DOROTHY RA MA SEDDON

Order this book online at www.trafford.com
or email orders@trafford.com

Most Trafford titles are also available at major online book retailers.

Printed in the United States of America.

ISBN: 978-1-4269-9387-9 (sc)
ISBN: 978-1-4269-9388-6 (e)

Library of Congress Control Number: 2011915969

Trafford rev. 10/24/2011

 www.trafford.com

North America & international
toll-free: 1 888 232 4444 (USA & Canada)
phone: 250 383 6864 ♦ fax: 812 355 4082

Books by Ruby Nari Mayo

The Catalysts, Book 1
True Heart, Book 2

Echo of a Dream
(available on www.dream-catcher.us)

Coming soon

The Quest, Book 3

Followed by Future Books

Blue Feather, Book 4
The Search, Book 5
Skye-Child, Book 6
Son of None, Book 7
Red Wing, Book 8

Dedication

To all the Light Masters and World Servers, thank you for your dedication and sacrifice for the benefit of advancing human consciousness. To our beloved Lord Adonis and the Advanced Light Masters, thank you for blessing our lives with service.

Introduction

Here is the awesome journey of Master Dorothy Ra Ma Seddon and Master Ruby Nariananda Mayo who have worked for eighteen years under the direction of Lord Adonis and other supportive Light Masters, in order to etherically and sometimes physically, plant crystals on the mountains of western America, Mexico, Canada and in other vital places, in order to form the awesome Crystal Grid.

It sounds like science fiction, but their story is very real, and as we all know, truth is stranger than fiction. Nothing like this Grid has been formed since the development of the Consciousness Grid, formed millenniums ago. The Crystal Grid has incorporated all other grids, each one holding their unique influences. Combined now into the Crystal Grid, they are generating powerful positive energies of Light and Love to influence and change human consciousness by providing ways to erase negative programming and increase spiritual awareness.

Foreword

I am Lord Adonis, a Light Master working with a selection of Light Masters who are developing the Crystal Grid. The description of Me by *Dr. Joshua Stone is accurate to a large degree, however, I do not choose to glorify self, but to glorify the individual efforts of the many people who, out of faith and service, have worked so hard to accomplish so much for the greater good of humanity.

*Exerts from the book, *"The Complete Ascension Manual"* published in 1994, by Dr. Joshua Stone.

Quote: "Adonis is a great and glorious being. He is considered the best in the universe at what he does. He embodies the heart focus of the universe. He is the keeper of the Christ Light within each soul in the universe.

We are not just working for the Earth; we are working, in reality, for the galaxy. To work just for the Earth would be selfish. In truth, we are creators working for a Universal goal, not just an Earth-centered or personality-centered goal. Call on Adonis for help, for we are very blessed to have him so available at this time." Unquote.

"I, Adonis, and My companions, come from the Planet Venus and represent the Love Energy that will influence changes necessary for the Earth's human survival. I have visited Earth many times in the past, preparing in stages the plan for this final grid, so that it could be implemented in this time of great events.

The concept for the Crystal Grid took very, very, long periods of time from the planning stage, to development, to finalization. Perfect timing was called for in bringing this powerful grid to Earth; timing that would culminate in a world-wide web of Light that would enhance the Powerful Love and Light Energies, along with all the assisting energies, would open humanity's consciousness to the full potential of the human race.

The purpose of the Crystal Grid is to assist and promote growth and change and help evolve people into the fifth dimension. This grid will also help the Feminine Cycle of Energy balance with the Masculine Cycle of Energy, as it must, in order to change the direction away from war and violence as a way to resolve political and religious differences in the world. If these negative forces are allowed to continue it will eventually lead to the Planet Earth's extinction. It is sufficient to say that We, as Evolved Masters of Light collective, are present on Earth, Mid-World and Heaven to assist humanity and not to accrue honors to Ourselves.

We chose Nariananda as the person through whom We speak as she is and was a Master and part of our assemblage, as was Dorothy Ra Ma Seddon, in other worlds. With these two courageous women, We have been successful in launching into completion the Crystal Grid in alliance with other Light Masters working in unison with their chosen correspondents. This has been a united effort and this Crystal Grid will be the last one created for Earth.

You might ask why did We choose women to do such vitally important work? It is written that women (the Feminine Energy) will save the world in this time of battle between the Light and the dark forces. The dark forces are turmoil, terrorism, death and chaos. These two women more than qualified for the service of such magnitude.

Their coming together in this lifetime was another demonstration of exquisite timing. In 1993 they began their journey of planting crystals upon designated mountains under Our command, and following Our guidance and direction, they did so. They have served Us and humanity well. The task, the energy, the time, the effort, and the money, it has taken them to complete Our portion of the web, was and is an immeasurable sacrifice on their part. They did this work under the vow of silence, for the building of the web of Light had to be done under cover, so as not to alert the dark forces and impede Our Masters in accomplishing the Great Purpose.

Light Masters around the world were working with Their world servers at the same time. It took eighteen years to finally complete the Crystal Grid. The final connection, the joining together of these other grids to complete The Crystal Grid were made by US and anchored in Mt. Shasta, which holds the OM Crystal. Now the Crystal Grid is fully activated and energized to help bring humanity's collective consciousness into a higher and more elevated state of spirit and mind.

The Crystal Grid is serving humanity at last and bringing about vast changes to the world. There will be chaos before the new beginnings can come into being since there will be resistances to changing the world's concept of behavior. The cup must be emptied before it can be filled with the new. The old structures of thought, old structures of beliefs, and old political and governmental barriers must be changed, and thus open to the new constructive energy that will unite people in peace, goodwill, and brotherhood with respect for all.

Time has escalated and time is noticeably collapsing, thus bringing about the new Heaven and the new Earth. You are all blessed to be witness to the mighty change that will have humanity triumph over the dark forces; dark forces that force people into slavery, killing the light workers, and all who would oppose them.

The Crystal Grid is empowered to act for the good and advancement and the liberty of all mankind so that peace and goodwill will be the energy of the Earth.

Our beloved Nariananda and our beloved Ra Ma have served above and beyond the call of duty.

It is with great love WE, the Light Masters, thank them for their sacrifices. The time for secrecy is past. It is time for the revelation.

Lord Adonis

Preface

Ruby Nariananda Mayo and Dorothy Ra Ma Seddon

Our lives didn't start out destined to be experienced as incredible journeys, or to experience incredible happenings, or helping to influence and change human consciousness. After all, we were just ordinary women, or so we believed. Everything appeared to be quite normal in the beginning of our lives. Like most people, we lived regular childhoods, doing regular things, like school, marriages, children, jobs; lives with the associated dramas and traumas of living.

Now we know many people that have and are living incredible lives; you can read about them or see them on television. They are exceptional people. Incredible lives happened to other people, don't they? But never in our wildest dreams did we imagine we would be one of them. However, we were wrong; it happened to us.

When did our 'ordinary' life stop and the extraordinary one kick in? For Dorothy it was meeting Cliff, the man who was destined to be her second husband. That too was to prove a vital part of the future work on the Crystal Grid. After Cliff's death, the following ten years Dorothy traveled the world, meeting people, family and establishing her winter home in Yuma, Arizona.

For Ruby, it was when she divorced and moved with her children to Arizona. For Ruby it was healing, absorbing the Ageless Wisdom, disciplined meditation and the meeting with Lord Adonis, a Light Master followed by the years being instructed by him.

We each began a new cycle without really knowing that we were going to be embarking on that *incredible part of our lives* in a very short time.

Ah, the happening; in 1992 Dorothy met me, because I was a Reiki Master living in Phoenix, Arizona. She didn't know at the time that I channeled for Lord Adonis. Unknown to us that meeting would change our lives and send us off in a new direction as partners in this great purpose, we began to work on helping to form the powerful and awesome Crystal Grid. Needless to say, our spiritual growth became super-activated also. So now we'll begin with the beginning of our mutual turning points.

Dorothy is the eldest and a Canadian. Nariananda is nine years younger and is an American. Dorothy is short and chubby, Nari is tall and slender. Dorothy, is an Earth Master and has more earth energies, thus she's more grounded. Nari, being from Venus, has a problem in staying grounded. She also has problems with her health. Dorothy is an introvert, Nari is an extravert. Dorothy has experience and proficiency in the field of finance, while Nari has experience in the field of metaphysics and is very proficient in this area. Dorothy was born in Aries (fire energy) and Nari was born in Cancer (water energy). And so these two women, who are direct opposites, managed to take their dualities and make them into complements. A perfect balance was struck. That is how it was planned before they were born.

Epigraph

Radiant Rays
Walk the Way
Of Love, Truth and Light

Radiant Rays
Down the days
Gathering in God's Sight

Speak unto men,
Collect and gather in
Those for the day fate-ing

For the chosen ones
The work is done
Upon the Grid stand waiting.

Nariananda
April 21, 1988

(This poem just "dropped" in one afternoon as I was counseling a friend. I frantically scrambled to write it down. At that same time, I had a vision of the world encompassed with a web, like a net, and there were points of light where the lines of the web intersected. For the following six years I didn't understand what it meant. It wasn't until Dorothy and I started placing crystals on the mountains that I realized what the poem and the vision were all about. I was in awe.)

STEP 1

Prologue

Nari: Many people, at some point in their life, ask a vital question; what is the meaning of my life? They often begin questioning if their life has purpose? Are they happy with their life so far? Do they feel unfulfilled in some way? I suppose this would come under the heading of *'mid-life crisis.'* Personally, I would call it *'mid-life evaluation.'* I know there are jokes about this crucial time, as if taking the time to review one's life wasn't of vital importance.

Too many people put up with, *'this is just the way my life is.'* Perhaps they fear to make any changes for possible expansion and greater joy. I call this the, *'don't let me rock the boat,'* or *'better the devil I know than the one I don't,'* syndrome. I know, because I was a past master at both syndromes.

The first turning point arrived and my own search for the meaning of my life came after many years of an unfulfilled, meaningless marriage. There isn't any reason to go into the particulars; it was just a very unhappy state. I learned that the more one refuses to face the truth of a situation, the worse it gets, the heavier it gets, and that often leads to physical illnesses. It did for me. All the events, emotions, and fears I had suppressed and wouldn't deal with brought me to the point of complete despair; to a point where I would rather die than go on battling life as it presented itself. Willful-blindness to my situation had to come to an end.

I divorced and went to live in Arizona, with my children, where I worked to support us. I earnestly sought to recreate myself and establish a new life. I was also fighting illness that would often attack me with crippling pain. Of course, it was emotionally backed, nothing physically was wrong, according to the Mayo Clinic.

Crisis is the only way a soul/a person is forced to make changes, because if you hurt enough, if you are discontented enough, unhappy enough, you will change just to escape the pain. Choice is always present.

Another turning point arrived one night! A severe attack brought me to my knees with a blast of pain that finally broke me. In the following purge of giving up, I let go of all my opinions, all the conditioned responses of how life and marriage should be. I forgave my husband and let him go. I forgave everyone and everything, and even gave up what I thought was *reality*. I think I covered all the bases until I was completely empty in that one amazing, gigantic catharsis. In the next instance I was swept by a gentle but overwhelming peace that washed through my physical, mental and emotional bodies. It was so powerful that I collapsed to the floor. Blissfully, I lay there, *changed!* From that point on, I never again experienced that agonizing pain.

I began disciplined Transcendental Meditation to help continue the deep healing of all that hindered my expansion of my spirit/Self. And so this was the regime for the next eight years. Joy filled my life once more. By that time meditation had helped me reach a level of mind that was clearer than ever before. It helped with my writing, problem solving, and a general on-going satisfaction with life.

I was working in Sausalito, California in 1985. It was evening and I was meditating when I was visited by a radiant blue **Etheric Master**. I instinctively knew he was my spiritual teacher. I was thrilled as I had been searching the physical world for just the spiritual master for me, and here he was; only he was an etheric one, which didn't matter to me. He began to speak and I was shocked not to be able to hear him, because I am clairaudient as well as clairvoyant. After several attempts by this **Light Master** to break through to me, he disappeared. I was left alone in my room feeling that I had failed a great test.

Within a few days, my daughter called me. She is also a strong talent. She said she was meditating and decided to check up on me to see how I was doing. She saw me painting this huge canvas with pyramids, (I am also an artist). She said, "This huge, blue God-like man burst through your canvas and stood looking down at you. Mom, I think he wants to talk to you." I asked her if he'd told her how that was going to happen? She said no, his energy was so powerful that it knocked her right out of the vision.

So there I was, an etheric Master wanted to communicate with me and we were at an impasse. The following weekend, while visiting friends up in Sebastopol, I told my friend **C.** about the experience. He suggested channeling. I very much disliked the idea of giving myself over to an unknown spirit, an entity, to use my body while I was elsewhere. We worked out a compromise which would insure that I'd always be partially present and aware, with the right to quit any time I chose.

That day I met the **Lord Adonis** and He spoke. Was I amazed? You better believe I was. Remember, I'm half in trance and half present. When **C** asked Him if He was of the Light and the Christ Conscious, He said, "Yes, We serve **THE CHRIST**". **C** then asked what was his name? In my half-awake mind I was saying to myself, how should I know what his name is? You could have knocked me over with a feather when I heard His voice say, "My name is **Lord Adonis.**

Turning point! Well, talk about a life-changing event! This was, yet again, another major switch in direction for me. The following seven years were filled with teaching Reiki, and channeling to large groups of people. I was also learning and becoming my spiritual Self. In 1990 I moved back to Arizona.

Ah, now we come to another major turning point. I met Dorothy Seddon in 1992. Did I know she would become my spiritual-partner/sister and serve a great purpose? A purpose that the **Light Masters** and **Lord Adonis** had come to achieve through their Earthly light workers? Did Dorothy and I know we'd probably volunteered to be those workers long before we were born? No, I did not, nor did she.

When I first met Dorothy Seddon, did I know she was to prove so unique? Heavens no, she was just another Reiki student. Well, she wasn't, and that was soon proven. I gave Dorothy the Master Level of Reiki in 1993 and introduced her to **Lord Adonis**.

And thus began our work on the Crystal Grid for the next eighteen years under the guidance and direction of **Lord Adonis** and **Company,** meaning the other **Light Masters** attending Him.

Did Dorothy and I know what an incredible adventure we were about to embarking on in 1993? Of course not; or else we'd probably have said, "no, thank you," and gone in the opposite direction. However, we held up our hands and said, quite cheerfully, "We'll do it." Fortunately, neither one of us were talented in being able to read the crystal ball of the future. In this instance, ignorance was bliss; and thus we began the extensive travel, expense, time and energy placing crystals of designated mountains as directed.

The following eighteen years proved to be exciting, fulfilling and greatly rewarding to know we were serving humanity through helping **Lord Adonis** and other **Light Masters** to plan, structure, implement, and finally to join the individual parts of the etheric grids into unification around the Earth, called the **Crystal Grid.**

Now, Dorothy will tell you about those intervening years that led her to me and to This Great Teacher.

Dorothy: My affair with crystals began in my making the best of a bad bargain. I had long since retired from my accounting practice in British Columbia, Canada. I received a small crystal ball as payment for some accounting work I had done. I liked it and tried to learn how to use it, to no avail. It became a pretty ornament on my mantle.

I have always had an inquisitive mind so my love of reading was eclectic, and gave me glimpses into many fields. I have never been interested in the study of any one religion, although I have a smattering of knowledge of several. My mother was Catholic, so I was exposed to Catholicism, more than any other religion, in my formative years. However my father didn't believe in churches, so I wasn't indoctrinated with any church's versions of heaven or hell. I was raised with the sure knowledge that there is a **GOD** and taught to have principles and ethics of an honest life.

I didn't appreciate this up-bringing for many years, as all my peers had a church they belonged to. Well, I asked, why not me? I had no idea, until I became interested in metaphysics and knew what an advantage this lack of indoctrination was. *When we struggle to clear our own habitual thought patterns and habits, it is a distinct advantage not to have the rituals of religion with which to battle.*

For most of my sixty-odd years I had been content with the knowledge that there is A Source, A Creator, The

Light and Love of **God.** It doesn't matter by what name you call the Deity, **GOD** has a thousand names. For me, it is a knowing that there is SOMETHING that created us all.

I am aware that we have Guides, Angels, Spirits and other advanced souls who help guide us as we stumble through the lessons we have come to learn. How do I know this? The first direct experience I had was the knowledge that my marriage had been virtually over with for some time, but I didn't have the courage to break the bonds and move on. As I was bemoaning my fate, I received this clear message:

"Go now, we have someone else for you."

Even while I was shocked to hear this command so plainly, I didn't hesitate or debate with myself or IT. I immediately left my home that evening. Three days later I met Cliff, my future husband at a hot springs hotel.

This guidance may have come through an angel or my higher self; all I do know is that I asked for help and I got it. Asking for help, helps! We find that things work out for our highest and best good if we heed the guidance we are given from our inner knowingness (intuition). We may want things another way, but given time, when we can see more of the big picture, we don't have any regrets. At least I never have.

In my search for greater understanding, I have read many self-help books on inner healing. I have always been curious about the prophets, especially Edgar Cayce.

I like all kinds of psychic readers, palm readers, tea-cup readers, or any other form of manifestation of "other" knowledge.

While in Arizona in 1990 I was introduced to a very psychic lady, Germaine Kal. After I returned to Canada, Germaine sent me a single terminated seed crystal, together with a tape. She instructed me to do the following dedication.

I dedicate this crystal to universal purpose
From this moment on.
I undertake to utilize its energies
To benefit all living things.
For I am one with the creative source
And therefore one with all life forms.
That which I am I now activate
The life energy within this crystal
That its force may now be utilized
To serve universal purpose.
Dedicated by Dorothy, August 1990

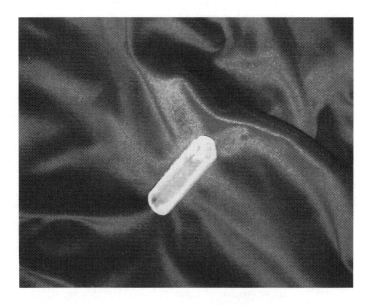

This crystal would prove to be essential in the on-going work that I would be embarking on in the near future.

I purchased a residence in Yuma, Arizona in 1988. From that year until 1993 I migrated with the snowbirds. A Snowbird is any person who migrates out of a winter climate into a warmer more comfortable and salubrious one and salubrious one as well; meaning a much warmer place to park for the winter.

A turning point for me: As I read an article on Reiki in the summer of 1992, I *knew* this was something that I wanted to have. Reiki is a healing modality that a student can be initiated into by a Master. It is a laying on of hands that channel healing and transformative energies to another person. I made arrangements with a Reiki Master in British Columbia and received the First Degree in the Usui System of Reiki.

As I was preparing to go to Arizona for five months that winter, I started to make inquiries concerning finding a Reiki Master in the Phoenix area. I was given the name of Reiki Master, Rev. Ruby Nariananda Mayo. We met in November of 1992 and Nari gave me the Second Degree Energies. After this initiation my spiritual life accelerated because Reiki Light opens the spiritual center and the Third Eye through which we visualize.

I met a number of people in Yuma who were involved in Reiki and in metaphysics and on one occasion I met Reiki Master Earleen. A few weeks later she got in touch with me. She told me she had received a message for me during her meditation. I was to be given the opportunity to learn about recognizing energies. This sounded exciting and it proved to be even more so.

As we walked in the desert Earleen declared that all snakes and poisonous insects would stay out of our aura. We proceeded to explore rabbit warrens, anthills, and miscellaneous animal habitats as well as the energy coming from plant life. She cautioned me to stay grounded at all times. As we returned to my home we walked around the back of the mobile home. A large salmon snake showed itself to us then quickly disappeared under my house. Could the snake have wanted us to see it? When we went into the house Earleen suggested that we put our hands on the floor to feel the snake's energy. As I did I received the impression that the snake was female and she had a family. Earleen thought the snake may have been attracted to the energy I created while doing Tai Chi. On making inquiries about the snake I was told that I was very lucky to have this salmon snake under my house for she would look after the mice and other rodents on the property.

While working on this book, I looked up the meaning of snake in the **"Medicine Cards"** by Jamie Sams and David Carson.

Quote: "The power of snake medicine is the power of creation, for it embodies sexuality, psychic energy, alchemy, reproduction and ascension (or immortality). The transmutation of the life-death-rebirth cycle is exemplified by the shedding of Snake's skin. It is the energy of wholeness, cosmic consciousness, and the ability to experience anything willingly and without resistance. On doing my chart on the nine Totem animals, Snake means *'Within.'*

Thoth, the Atlantian who later returned as Hermes and was the father of alchemy, used the symbology of two snakes intertwining around a sword to represent healing. Complete understanding and acceptance of the male and female within each organism creates a melding of the two into one thereby producing divine energy." Unquote.

Looking back, I would say this incident was very prophetic.

Time marched on and in March, 1993, Ruby Nariananda Mayo, (I shall refer to her as Nari from now on), gave me Reiki's Third Degree, the Master Teaching Degree. Then Nari introduced me to the **Lord Adonis**.

Little did I know, this was to become the beginning of our incredible journey.

The Mexican Adventure

Nari: Dorothy had gone back to Canada in the spring of 1993 and I was living in Phoenix searching for a job and sending out resumes. The heat of summer in June is fierce in the desert. Earlier that spring, I had helped to sell my mother's mobile home then packed her for her trip to Sandpoint, ID to live in a nice condo with my sister to look after her. Thus I was without a home for awhile.

I was temporarily staying with my son and his wife and was very anxious to get a job and into my own apartment. I was just returning home after another interview. I was feeling very frustrated, angry, and very hot because my A/C was failing. No matter how hard I was working to secure a job so I could live independent, I was failing.

Driving home that afternoon, I lost it. I screamed at the Universe, *"I want change now!"* then thought about the consequences of dragging an innocent person into my demand, so I quickly added, *"But only for the highest and best good of all concerned."* Fortunately, this tirade happened with my car's windows tightly closed, or it might have shocked a few people hearing a lone, manic woman screaming at nothing.

The next day I received a surprise phone call from Dorothy. "Nari, I received a message from my guides. I'm to fly down to Arizona and pick you up. We're supposed to go to Yuma together."

I was in shock! Oh, wow, was this the universe's way of answering my demand? Talk about instant response! Well, it would get me out of Phoenix, out of my job problem temporarily, and do something different. And perhaps this was an answer as to why I hadn't been able to secure a job. Well, okay, I felt good about this switch and change, but couldn't help wondering what this trip was going to be about. I just bet **Lord Adonis** had His fingers in our pie!

Two days later Dorothy arrived. Because my car had lost its A/C, and trust me, you don't want to drive through the desert in summer without A/C. So Dorothy rented a car and the next day we left for Yuma and her winter home.

Half way there, I said, "Please pull over, Dorothy, I'm getting a message."

She did and turned off the engine. In the silence that surrounded us, we looked out on the dry desert scene. Above us we could see a circling hawk. Usually, according to Native Americans, this meant there was definite a message coming, and sure enough, **Lord Adonis** gave the answer.

"Dorothy," I said, "I know you told me that you were to place a crystal on a mountain, but there's more to it than just that. You'll be placing many crystals on many mountains. I'm not sure what this means, but **He** will talk to us later."

Dorothy looked surprised, but didn't question me. "Well, I wonder what this is all about. This should be interesting, don't you think?"

We were to learn quickly that *that* was a wowzier of under statement We drove on to Yuma.

It's amazing to me how certain experiences stick in your memory. It didn't seem to matter how long ago they took place; they're stuck in your mind like glue.

The trip into Mexico was one of those memorable experiences. June, 1993 found Dorothy and I in Yuma,

Arizona, which is divided from California by the Colorado River. Yuma sits right on the border of Arizona and California.

Dorothy and I had the weekend free while we waited for her car to be serviced. We still had the rental car and nothing much to do. We decided to drive 25 miles and cross the Mexican border to San Luis, and go shopping.

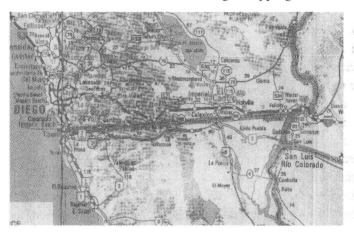

Arriving in San Luis was easy; it was a straight 25 miles down the road. Well, we shopped and looked around the town for a while, thoroughly enjoying ourselves. As it was a very hot day, we bought a six pack of Mexican beer, which we were going to take back to the states with us. Since we had the whole weekend ahead of us Dorothy suggested we head west to Mexicali Mexico, which was only about 73 miles and go over the border into California at Calexico and on to El Centro, California and do more shopping.

Dorothy was driving us out of San Luis to catch the highway to Mexicali when I noticed that our gas gauge was half-way between a quarter and empty. I suggested that we gas up before leaving town. Dorothy said she never bought

Mexican gas and we had enough gas to get to California then we'd gas up.

So off we went, and drove, and drove….and drove some more. The dessert surrounding us was hot, empty and flat, except for occasional barren hills, rocks and not a house to be seen. The open road stretched out before us like an undulating snake. I eyed the gas gauge and saw it was now riding on red; that meant EMPTY!

I called Dorothy's attention to the gauge and she said, yes, she saw it and was worried too, but she was sure Mexicali was just around the hill as we'd come over fifty miles or there about.

It wasn't.

Now we were both severely worried. The dessert in the summertime is no place to be stranded without water, and that six-pack of beer certainly wouldn't last us very long. Besides this, we hadn't seen a car, truck or a bus since we left San Luis. Did I mention we hadn't seen any houses either? Yeah, we were worried!

When we came around a hill, miracle of miracles, we saw a large weather-beaten building with a number of junk cars off to one side. The old building was just sitting there in the middle of nothing but dessert. I don't remember seeing a tree. There was a bus stopped by the road. Well, it was civilization, and you can imagine our sigh of relief at the sight of that ugly old weathered building. At that moment it was more beautiful to us than the Taj Mahal.

As we drove into the yard we didn't see any gas pumps! Oh, Lordy! Well, we parked close to the porch which shaded the car somewhat. We talked about what we were going to do. Dorothy said she'd go talk to the bus driver while I went go into the store and question the proprietor.

When I entered the store, the coolness of the interior felt wonderful. Even that brief exposure to the intense sun was a bit much. I have a smattering of Spanish, a few words here and there, but hand-signs work amazingly well I found.

I asked the lady, "Senora, la carretera pasar por California?" and pointing in the direction we had been driving. She shook her head, "No, senora, Tejas." Texas! *Texas?* We were driving toward Texas on an empty tank of gas? Holy Mother of God! That had to be over 200 miles to the next town!

So I pointed back the way we came, and said softly, "La carretera a Arizona?" She nodded. I next asked her for gasoline, and she shook her head no. Just then Dorothy walked in and told me she couldn't make sense of what the bus driver said. I told her what I'd found out.

We both sat down at a table, this being a sort of lunchroom for people riding the bus. I say we sat, but collapse is more like it. There we were, out in the middle of the Sonora dessert in Mexico with no gas, no phone, and no idea as to what to do next.

Dorothy wanted to ask the senora what was the name of that mountain across the road from us. I told her to ask, ¿Esta se illama El Monte? Which means, "What is the mountain's name?" I told her to point anyway, which Dorothy did. The woman responded, "*La montaña se llama Picati.*" Its name was Mount Picati.

Dorothy returned and said, "This is to be the first mountain we're to put a crystal on." I checked with **Lord Adonis** and sure enough, she was right. Lordy the girl was intuitive!

Dorothy sat down and began to write then she read it to me. "This is the invocation we will use on all the mountains we place crystals on."

She and I walked across the large yard and over to the edge of the mountain. Here Dorothy placed a crystal.

This is the dedication that will be used for all the mountains crystals to come.

> *We call upon the Lords of Light, Love and Power*
> *And the Christ Matraiya in whose service*
> *We dedicate this mountain.*
> *We place a crystal upon this mountain's crest*
> *To radiate purification out to the Earth,*
> *To all Kingdoms and to humanity.*
> *This radiating crystal is to assist humans*
> *To raise their consciousness in preparation*
> *For the coming of the Christ. We declare this*
> *Mountain to be healed, empowered*
> *And linked to all other mountains*
> *Forming the Crystal Grid.*

Now how strange was this? Was it by *accident* we found the first mountain on which to place the very first crystal? Were we brought here on purpose? Obviously! Oh, my, what a dramatic beginning to our beginning adventure. Dorothy and I hoped they all weren't going to be like this. Little did we know, which is just as well, I suppose.

And so the very first crystal was planted in the formation of the Crystal Grid.

We sat at our little table and thought about our problem of what *do* we do now? We're still were out of gas and stuck. Well, nothing came to mind. The bus left. There was only one thing to do; get our beer out of the car since the establishment didn't sell beer, and order some food. Maybe one or both would kick-start our brains out of shock. So we ordered two burritos and drank a beer while eating and gazing out through the screen door at the heat waves coming off the dirt yard.

They were the best burritos I've ever eaten and served by a nice *little* old lady all of five foot nothing. In fact, they were so good we ordered two more. Whether it was the food or the cool beer, but my brain finally fired as I looked out at that side-yard full of used cars. These people had to have a car to get to town, didn't they? Hmm, at last, an idea!

I took $20 dollars out of my purse and walked over to the counter where the senora was standing. I smiled and showed her the money and said, *"Quiero cinco galones de adjetivo sin plomo gasolina por un esta de veinte dólares de Estados Unidos"*

She understood my less than perfect Spanish because she disappeared into the kitchen. I briefly saw four men sitting at a kitchen table.

Well, me and my $20 American dollars went back to the table and smiled at Dorothy, "We've got gas!" I said, and Dorothy laughed.

I think, back in 1993, the exchange rate was around 12 pesos to an American dollar. They came off with $240 pesos, minus the gas. Not a bad day's work for the men and certainly worth every penny to us. I felt no need to haggle on the price; just get the job done.

Within minutes four men trouped by the screen door carrying a white five-gallon bucket and a siphon hose. Yep, Dorothy and I grinned at each other, opened another beer, and toasted ourselves and waited. Five minutes later I walked out onto the porch and looked around. The men were over to the right siphoning gas out of a car. I walked over and said hello and looked in at the dash board. It said unleaded gas.

Just to make sure I asked the gentlemen, *"adjetivo sin plomo gasolina?"* They smiled and nodded.

"Bueno," I smiled. You bet it was good!

It wasn't long after that the men came back. I don't know why it took four of them to do the job, but what the heck, they probably didn't get to many crazy foreign women who happened to run out of gas at their establishment then pay them an outrageous amount of money for five gallons of gas. Of course, the plus factor was, we *were* entertainment too.

So Dorothy and I went out to join the men and entertain them with our form of communication. They politely showed us the full five-gallon can and then proceeded to pour it through a funnel into our gas tank. What a lovely sight that was!

Meanwhile, with our broken Spanish and their broken English, plus hand gestures, well, all in all, we had a great conversation. They wanted to know all about Canada. *Estaba muy frio alli? (*was it awfully cold there?) It was a challenge to describe Canada to them, at least I tried, and I think we got some understanding across. However, I'm not sure that they still didn't believe that Dorothy lives with the polar bears. Where I lived held no interest as they knew about Arizona.

We finally said, *"Muchas gracias, hasta luego, via con dios,"* waved, and took off. They all were such very, very good people. They probably talked about the crazy foreign women for months that had run out of gas and paid a fortune for so little. Price is always relative to the need. They got a big deal and we got what we needed. Everyone was happy.

Dorothy and I talked about it on our way back to San Luis. You know, not once did we fear for our lives, or feel threatened, or worried about being robbed, killed and buried in the dessert. After all, no one knew where we had gone in the first place. We were truly lost.

Yes, we had been worried as to how we were going to get out of this fix we were in, but we were never afraid of the people.

We crossed the border into the U.S. and immediately stopped at the first gas station and filled up. Dorothy and I made a pact, never to let the gas tank get below half full again. We kept that vow.

It would never do to over-tax our guardian angels by repeating the same stupid mistake that apparently wasn't a mistake after all. *Well, it wasn't!*

You can't tell me our guardian angels weren't working overtime.

Following the Crystal Path

Looking back over this next episode, it's hard to believe that Dorothy and I simply accepted the strangeness of putting crystals on the mountains for the **Light Masters**. Perhaps our minds were cloaked from questioning the rationality of these actions so that we could perform them without affecting the crystals with our negative thinking. We were told by **Lord Adonis** not to tell anyone what we were doing. I think this was to prevent other people from trying to convince us that we were crazy; thus stopping us from completing our segment of the Grid.

Step by step we were lead to do the work. Well, our next adventure began right after we returned from Mexico. Dorothy and I took off for California in her big Oldsmobile. Granted, it wasn't a new car, I think it was a 1978, but it was a nice one that Dorothy left in Yuma for her use during the winters.

I was driving, cruising down Hwy 8 toward San Diego at a good clip, slightly over the speed-limit as I recall, maybe doing 75-80 when, BAM, the left front tire blew, spewing rubber all over the road. It's amazing how much strength one can call up in sudden emergencies. *I became Superwoman!* Fortunately, I was able to slowly pull the car over to the side of the road.

I think Dorothy and I spent a good ten minutes just getting our heart-rates back to normal. I finally got out to check the tire and was astonished to see the tire was still inflated. There it sat, on its webbing, without a shred of rubber to cover its nakedness. Now that was indeed a miracle. Obviously, our guardian angels were still keeping us safe.

I turned on the flashers and creped slowly, at 20 miles an hour, down the freeway into El Centro. We pulled off the freeway, down the off-ramp and found a Firestone Garage straight ahead of us. Talk about an answered prayer!

We pulled in and Dorothy got out. The man asked what he could do for her and she said, "I want four new, four-ply tires and trash these others." Dorothy was very upset as those retreads weren't that old, but safety first was her motto, and I was all for that.

Once back on the road, we both breathed a sigh of relief. It has been a close call and we were deeply grateful for the protection.

As we passed Mt. Laguna, we got the word to place a crystal on that mountain which of course, we did. Driving through San Diego we took the 5 Freeway north and got off on the 405 heading for Huntington Beach where my daughter and her family lived. After a brief overnight visit, Dorothy and I headed east for Sedona, our next port of call.

Now, I know it will appears strange to our readers that we left Yuma, Arizona, one day and drove to place a crystal on a California mountain near San Diego, drove north almost to L.A, then the next day, headed back east to northern Arizona. Please remember we were following **Lord Adonis's** *directions and He wanted these mountains to be given crystals in a particular order. Why? Well, I really never understood the why, ours was just to DO.*

We spent the night in Flagstaff, Arizona then drove down to Sedona the next morning. Sedona is simply an awesomely beautiful area; red rocks, high mesas, green valleys and chock-full of great energies. We had a dedication to do while there.

The Sedona Airport is up on a high mesa overlooking the area. There is a highly energized vortex on Airport and we walked out to where we could feel the energy and placed a crystal there. Then we dedicated ourselves to the work of the **Light Masters** and to serving **GOD'S WILL**. It was a profound moment that had us feeling so connected that there would be no breaking those vows.

We drove back north to Flagstaff and placed another crystal on the San Francisco Peaks, a holy mountain and home to the Kachinas, the Gods, according to the Native Americans.

So now we were ready to head for Las Vegas, Nevada and north to Canada, eventually. Well, best laid plans are just hunky-dory, except when the hand of fate or the **Light Masters** switch plans on us. In Kingman, Arizona we had a fan belt break. Okay we fixed that. Then within a few miles the transmission began to make funny noises. Having car trouble in a small town isn't a good thing, so we decided to go back to Phoenix and get my car and fix the A/C and store Dorothy's Oldsmobile. We made it before we broke anything important.

Once we had the A/C fixed, we would be all set. Of course, while we waited, we placed crystals on Camelback Mountain in Phoenix and on the Superstition Mountains which are east of Phoenix. That's what was next on the **Light Masters** agenda. Mission accomplished, and three days later we finally headed for Las Vegas, Nevada.

Once we arrived we got a hotel room and then drove up to Mt. Charles where we placed a crystal. We passed a pleasant evening having a nice dinner, looking around, and doing a little gambling; little is the operate word, as no one was going to be paying our expense account.

Well, the word came from **Lord Adonis** that we were to head for San Francisco. That filled out the day nicely for it's quite a long drive. Again we stayed overnight then visited Mt. Tam and put a crystal up there. I guess that was all for the S.F. area, so we kept driving north Highway 5. When Mt. Shasta came into view I told Dorothy the story of my visiting the mountain in 1982 and the lovely crystal-cluster I left high on the mountain for the **Light Masters** abiding there. Still, we were directed to place another crystal on the mountain. I don't know why the **Light Masters** couldn't have used the one I had left there years ago, but to obey is all, I guess. Funny, I never asked **Lord Adonis** about that.

Dorothy informed me that this completed the seven mountains in the first grid and they were now connected to Mt. Shasta. Hmm, I wonder how she knew to do that? That girl had to be psychic. I guess that's why we are partners in this endeavor.

From Dorothy's notes: "As this work progressed we were given seven inter-connecting mountains and instructions for placing the crystals on these mountains with a timer so they could be activated when all crystals in the grid were in place. In addition, as we completed each grid of seven mountains, we were to connect it to the existing grids and to Mt. Shasta."

We worked our way north to Canada and ended our journey by placing a crystal on Mt. Cheam in Chilliwack, B.C., an altogether awesome mountain, in view of Dorothy's home town.

I boarded a plane for Salt Lake, Utah on the next adventure. I was instructed to place a crystal on King's Peak (13,528 ft.) It's part of the Wasatch Mountain Range, which is part of the Rocky Mountains. I flew back to Vancouver, B. C. later that afternoon.

Meanwhile Dorothy flew to Calgary for a family gathering. We had made arrangements to meet in Calgary, Alberta, in a week so I decided to drive over to Sandpoint, Idaho and visit my mother. After a nice visit I drove through Glacier National Park in Montana. As I drove up through a mountain pass called, 'Going to the Sunset Highway', or Logan's Pass, I placed a beautiful crystal there. I might have gotten carried away with all the gorgeous mountains around me and put a few here and there, maybe they wouldn't be used in the Crystal Grid, but I'm sure they would benefit the environment in some way.

I picked Dorothy up at the hotel in Calgary, Alberta and we drove back west placing a crystal on Mt. Aylmer before driving into Banff National Park. The next day we drove north on the Parkway to Mt. Robson, then back to Highway 1 to get to Mt. Revelstoke.

By the time we arrived back in Chilliwack, B.C., we were both exhausted. We rested a few days before Dorothy had to fly to Prince Rupert, which is north along the inland waterway to Alaska. She placed a crystal on Mt. Faucet.

Back home in Chilliwack, B.C. again, we sat down and figured out how many crystals we had blessed the mountains with. It turned out to be 21 crystals in place and that completed this phase of the formation. Yes, it was a great accomplishment and we treated ourselves to a nice celebration dinner out on the town. After all, all work and no play makes for very unhappy women.

I began to work on my book that was going to be a series of articles and insights I was taking from my journals, which I had written over the years.

Now here's a story for you, another coincidence?

I had transcribed about ten pages and was pleased with the work so far. One morning I was having coffee when Dorothy came into the kitchen. (We later called this Dorothy's potty meditation). She said, "Nari, that isn't the book you're supposed to write. Come with me." Mystified, I followed her upstairs to her office, where she sat me down in front of her computer, gave me a few instructions then said, "Write."

She walked out of the room and closed the door leaving me facing a blank screen and a blinking cursor. How intimidating is that, I ask you? It's all very well to say, 'write,' but write what? I didn't have a clue! I'm not sure how long I sat there, probably just five or ten minutes, but it seemed like hours. I finally decided to place my hands on the keyboard and meditate. At least I wouldn't be wasting my time. Within minutes I 'heard,'

> **In the beginning**
> **We came to Earth as spirits**
> **To enjoy this paradise, God's Garden....**

I completed one page, and it seemed to be an introduction of some sort. But when I read it, I thought, Good Lord, am I to write the creation of the world?

I waited and again I 'heard',

> **One day,**
> **at the gate of a small town**
> **in northern India,**
> **a stranger appeared.**
> **She walked quietly through the street**
> **into the town's central plaza**
> **where an Ancient Bodhi Tree grew**
> **in isolated splendor.**
> **She sat down in its shade and meditated....**

When I had completed that first chapter, I was thrilled so I printed it out and took it downstairs for my friends to read.

They thought it was beautiful and asked me what happens next?

Well, how should I know, for goodness sake, and I really didn't! As far as I knew this might be all there was. So each day, for the next fourteen days, I'd listen and wrote one or two chapters. I must say it was exciting. It wasn't until I was in the middle of chapter twelve that I realized I was writing about a past life of mine because I remembered a nightmare I'd had all my life about falling off a bridge and being swept away by the river. So my friend Dorothy was right on; this was the book I was supposed to write. I called it, "Echo of a Dream."

Dorothy often amazes me with her sudden insights. "Echo of a Dream" wasn't to be published until 2004, as these intervening years were very busy for both Dorothy and me.

The rest of that summer I spent in Chilliwack teaching our dear friend, J, and instructing Dorothy, in Reiki. In September I left Canada and drove to Huntington Beach, California to stay with my daughter for a while.

Now here's another amazing event that was to figure strongly in what would take place in our very near future. As with all these *"coincidences,"* they were significant in the ongoing process of forming the Crystal Grid.

Dorothy: Back in 1990 I took an Elder Hostel trip to Ottawa, Canada where I met a charming couple from Hawaii, who I will call Mr. & Mrs. **H.** for privacy sake. In the ensuing friendship they asked me if I would like to house-sit in Kailua, Oahu, Hawaii. They explained that they were looking for a reliable person to house-sit. This was for their neighbors on their street, when they traveled. I told them that I had a winter home in Yuma at the time, but maybe later. I gave them my card.

We kept in touch over the following years. In August of 1993 I received a letter from the **Hs**, asking if I would be available to take a house-sitting job from December 19th, to February 21, 1994. As I was in the process of selling my winter home in Yuma, I told them I'd be free to take this on. I contacted Nari in California and told her about the job offer. She had no trouble agreeing that a vacation in the sun was just what the doctor ordered. So I fired off a letter to Hawaii agreeing to the house-sitting arrangement.

I flew to Phoenix at the end of September and my friend from Wickenburg met me. He drove me to where I had stored my Oldsmobile, and after we replaced the battery, I carefully drove to Wickenburg, where his mechanic friend replaced the transmission. Within a few days I was off to Yuma to pack, clean the house and complete the paper work on the sale. A question arose; what would Nari and I do for two months from the middle of October until we left for Hawaii in December? Consulting with Nari, we decided to rent an apartment in Las Vegas for this period.

Nari: When Dorothy called me and invited me to go with her to Hawaii for two months I was thrilled. Who wouldn't be happy to spend two months basking in the sun and drink an occasional Mai Tai? Well, basking in the sun was right down my alley. I drove to Yuma and helped Dorothy pack her household goods into a trailer. Since I had the younger Oldsmobile, I pulled the trailer with Dorothy following me in her car. After we arrived in Las Vegas we put Dorothy's household goods in storage then we rented a motel-apartment for the time we needed before leaving for Hawaii in December.

Dorothy: While in Las Vegas I was inspired to purchase three books that Katrina Raphaell had published. I understood that I was not to study about crystals, but use these books as references. With time on my hands I browsed through them and I was completely intrigued by the chapter on the Earthkeepers, huge crystals, and in particular the one on Kauai.

Before we left for Hawaii, **Lord Adonis** connected me to the Crystal Grid. Nari was already connected through her association with Him.

Nari: While we were in Las Vegas, our friend **J**, came down from Canada for a visit. **J** and I drove up to Sedona, Arizona for a two-day seminar with Torkum Saraydarian, my Spiritual Teacher and an Ageless Wisdom Master. Afterward we drove back to Las Vegas to join Dorothy. While driving toward Flagstaff on Hwy 40, we turned off to buy gas at Williams and found a cute little souvenir shop. I wanted to take Dorothy a gift and as I was looking around I saw this cute little pewter elephant. I've always loved pewter, so I bought it. I had no idea that it would be one of those articles that would be needed later.

A week later, Dorothy and I put **J** on a plane for Canada. It had been a lovely visit.

In December, after storing Dorothy's car, we left Las Vegas and drove to Huntington Beach, California to stay with my daughter for a few days until we caught the plane out of Los Angeles for Hawaii on December 19, 1993.

Our next adventure was on. Little did we know what that was going to become. The **Light Masters** certainly knew how to keep secrets and spring surprises. Good thing Dorothy and I were resilient.

STEP 2

Introduction
by Lord Adonis

Now we begin to bring the various components of the Crystal Grid together. We will regress a little into the sequences of events that appeared to be separate and diverse, and not of any great connection to the work I and my fellow Masters were about to perform. Yet these components were vital to the ongoing development of the Crystal Grid.

In 1982, Nari was on her way north through California to visit her parents in Idaho. Inspired by the recent knowledge of Light Masters that dwelled upon and in Mt. Shasta, she and her friends drove up the mountain and parked near the top. They proceeded to walk a great distance up closer to the crest. In a field of rock they separated. Nari had taken a large double-crystal cluster with her as an offering to these Light Masters. The field of rocks held a number of other offerings, none of which had ever been touched by visitors. After meditating for a while, Nari placed her crystal-cluster on a flat rock and walked away. At that time she didn't have any knowledge that Mt. Shasta had the OM Crystal buried in its base. This act was a link to the future activities.

In 1985 we contacted Nari and formed a partnership with her as our channel.

In 1986 Gurudevaubramuniyaswami, Master of the Hindu temple in Kauai, Hawaii, grew a crystal *which he then gave to *Almitra Zion and sent her to Arkansas to procure an Earthkeeper, a giant Crystal.*

In 1987 the Earthkeeper was in place in the Hindu Temple in time for the Harmonic Convergence. The Earthkeeper, the Isis Crystal, would be pivotal and vital to the work of establishing the Crystal Grid.

In 1990 Dorothy met a couple from Hawaii that would be an important key to unlocking the Earthkeeper in the next cycle of events. This key, if not turned, would prove a large hindrance to Our Plans for Hawaii.

In 1992, Dorothy Seddon meets our channel and Reiki Master, Ruby Nari Mayo.

In 1993 was the initiation of Dorothy Seddon into the Master Degree of Reiki and Our introduction to her. The next step for placing of crystals upon the mountains could now begin.

All these events were planned and executed accordingly. All were significant factors necessary to the building of the Crystal Grid.

So beloveds continue with the journey to Hawaii. Such are the importance of these quiet coincidences to the overall vital performance.

Lord Adonis

Hawaii

Nari: We flew from Los Angeles to Honolulu on December 19, 1993 and were met by Dorothy's friends, the Haywards. That evening and we settled into our residence just a few houses away from their house in Kailua on the Island of Oahu. It was a lovely bungalow on the canal with the ducks as our close neighbors. Besides house-sitting, we had the pleasure of caring for a sweet, golden Labrador dog. I must admit, I was ill when we flew into Honolulu and it took me a week to recover from the flu. God bless Dorothy for her care. This wasn't the way I wanted to begin a lovely sojourn in paradise, but I healed quickly in the warmth of Hawaii.

Dorothy and I got to explore and roam around enjoying the novelty and the great beauty of the Island, not to mention the sunny weather. New Year's Eve, as they have it in Hawaii, means lots, and lots, and extreme loads of fireworks. *Lordy, it sounded like World War 111 and lasted for hours!* I stayed home with the dog because I don't like loud noise and neither did he. Brave Dorothy and the Haywards went down to Honolulu and celebrated the New Year in. I have no liking for large crowd of people, besides the poor dog was traumatized by the noise, so someone had to stay with him so he wouldn't have a nervous breakdown, or me either, for that matter.

Dorothy: In January I phoned the number listed in the back of one the books of Katrina's to inquire about how to find the Hindu Temple that housed the Earthkeeper. The woman who answered the phone gave me the directions and then asked if I would be there for the Palladium Alignment on January 21st? Not knowing anything about the importance of this date, I said "No". However, the best laid plans of mice and man found us at the temple in Kauai on that day; another coincidence? Later Nari said that the **Light Masters** were good at keeping secrets and presenting sudden surprises with little warning. So I guess we shouldn't have been surprised. It takes a while to get used to being blind-sided even in the nicest way.

While in Hawaii **Lord Adonis** gave us a number of grids to complete and the first one was to place a crystal on Mt. Haleakala on Maui. We had no prior knowledge why this mountain was to be the first mountain in Hawaii to be so crystallized that it was apparently vital to the ongoing formation of the Crystal Grid. It was only later that we could see the pattern.

On January 11, 1994, I received this message while meditating: *"It is difficult to explain the work you will be doing. It will be easier when you actually get started. The way of the Spirit is with you. There will be a time for everything. You are to come back to Hawaii in May! You will see the Earthkeeper, as it is a key to the hierarchy and will benefit all mankind. Part of your purpose is unfolding its message. Your knowledge is required in the total unfolding of the Earthkeeper's purpose. This will be revealed to you as you progress in your work with the Earthkeeper."*

January 21, 1994, the day of the Palladium Alignment, Nari and I left for Kauai. I did not plan this trip for this particular date, but obviously the **Light Masters** did. While flying over to Kauai we could see Mt. Haleakala in the distance and, following **Lord Adonis's** instruction, we placed a crystal on its peak.

Nari: We arrived in Kauai, which is mountainous, and saw the remains of the hurricane damage, but driving up into the mountains toward the Temple we didn't see much damage there at all. Arriving at the Hindu Temple we parked and walked into the beautiful serene grounds surrounding the Temple's entrance. It was so quiet with only the birds singing in the trees.

We stopped at the entrance and took off our shoes before stepping into the temple itself. And there it sat; this awesome crystal, the Earthkeeper.

Dorothy: We beheld the Earthkeeper sitting on a dais in the nave of the temple and it was something extra special to see and feel. The Earthkeeper stands 39 inches high and weighs 700 pounds. It is a single terminated crystal. It is the focal point of the temple. The peace, tranquility and love I felt there is somehow very hard to describe. *IT JUST IS:*

Nari: Everyone has a different reaction to this magnificent crystal I'm sure. Mine was an unbelievable sense of "presence" as though we were facing an ancient receptacle of wisdom; very profound and emitting an energy of serenity and love. It was indeed, an overwhelming and unique experience. I loved it.

Dorothy: Nari and I meditated with the monk who was sitting on the floor at the side of the Earthkeeper. I was very aware that **Lord Adonis** was present, so there were three of us along with the monk paying homage to the Earthkeeper. When this was over the monk introduced himself as Gurudeva, Master of the Hindu Temple. He asked how we had found the Temple. I explained that the lady who answered the phone gave us directions. He looked at me with a quizzical look on his face and said, "This is a monastery. There are no females in this residence". Well, what could I say about that. It was a woman to whom I had spoken. More divine guidance by the **Light Masters?**

I would like to formally introduce Satguru Sivaya Subramuniyaswami, affectionately known as Gurudeva. He lived from 1927 to 2001. Kauai's Hindu Monastery was founded by Satguru Sivaya Subramuniyaswami, or Gurudeva, in 1970.

Once in a while on this Earth there arises a soul who, by living his tradition rightly and wholly perfects his path and becomes a light to the world. Gurudeva was such a being, a living example of awakening and wisdom, a leader recognized worldwide as one of Hinduism's foremost ministers.

For over five decades Gurudeva taught Hinduism to Hindus and seekers from all faiths. Gurudeva was lauded as one of the strictest and most traditional gurus in the world. His Hindu Church nurtures its membership and local missions on five continents.

In the last years of his life Gurudeva was a key member of Vision Kauai 2020, a small group of community leaders that includes the Mayor, former Mayor and Country Council Members. They met monthly to fashion the Island's future for twenty years ahead, based on moral and spiritual values.

If you asked people who know Gurudeva what was so special about him, they may point to his great peace, presence and centeredness, to his incredible power to inspire others toward their highest Self, to change their lives in ways that are otherwise impossible, to be an unfailing light on their path, to be a voice of Indian Spiritual Life, to bring the best of the East and the best of the West together, to be a father and mother to all who draw near, a living example of the pure path taught by his guru and followed by his devoted shishyas.

On August 2000, he received the prestigious *United Nations U Thant Peace Award* in New York (previously bestowed on the Dali Lama, Nelson Mandela, Mikhail Gorbachev, Pope John Paul 11 and Mother Teresa). He addressed 1,200 spiritual leaders gathered for the UN millennium Peace Summit, with the message, "For peace in the world, stop the war at home." Excerpt from a 'From a Short Biography.' **www.himalayanacademy.com**

Lord Adonis wanted me to mentally connect the three of us to the Earthkeeper and IT to the Crystal Grid, as we were all three present at the same time. I did so.

(I had to wonder why Lord Adonis wanted us to be connected to the Earthkeeper, but I did it. No doubt that I would be given an understanding if it was necessary to know.)

We thanked Gurudeva and took our leave, arriving back in Honolulu the same day. On the plane returning to Honolulu, I placed, in the etheric, a crystal in Japan, Jamaica, and New Guinea. Followed by Columbia, San Felipe, Mexico, with Mt. Haleakala and the Earthkeeper on Kauai making a total of seven, this grid was connected to Mt. Shasta.

In her book, "A Crystal Journey," published in 1991, Amitra Zion tells of being commissioned by Gurudeva to procure a Crystal for the temple. She tells of how Gurudeva gave her a crystal he had grown for this purpose. She was to take this crystal with her to Arkansas. It would tell her when she had found the right Earthkeeper for the Hindu Temple. Gurudeva requested that the crystal be in Hawaii for the Harmonic Convergence that was to take place in August of 1987.

Before we left Hawaii, in February, of 1994, I was made aware that I must be here to awaken the Earthkeeper in the Hindu Temple in Kauai in May. How intimidating is that?

I had read about the process in *Crystal Healing" by Katrina Raphaell. She has a section on this process, page 162, where she outlines the procedure for awakening these sleeping giants. The Earthkeepers, as Katrina has written, are ancient formations brought to Earth millions of years ago. Their knowledge, contained within their crystalline depths, was available to the first people who brought them to Earth. So it is to be again. The Earthkeepers are here to remind us of our origins. The one on Kauai will be first to awaken. Its message will be felt throughout the Cosmos. Katrina talks about the fact that twenty-one people, of like mind, need to be on hand for the ceremony.

Faced with the difficulty of having twenty-one people in Kauai at the same time, in this day and age, was practically impossible. No Way! Fortunately my guides told me that when I have twenty-one people who agreed to have me represent them in Kauai, then the ceremony could take place. *No easy task, but doable!* As luck or someone else's plan, I was asked to house-sit in May on the same street. How convenient was that?

Arriving back in California, Nari and I proceeded east. l placed crystals on a number of mountains in Mexico This was done from the highest point of the pass from San Diego. We then proceeded to Albuquerque where I placed a number of crystals on mountains in Texas, New Mexico and Colorado. **Lord Adonis** told us that the grid was now stronger. Our clearings were progressing and our spiritual power was stronger. I could place the crystals from a greater distance now which helped facilitate the completion of our section of the grid. Nari and I were both changing rapidly and expanding consciously. I believe that this accelerated pace was necessary in order to do the high volume of work expected of us.

We returned to Las Vegas and gathered up my storage and rented a trailer. Nari hauled the rented trailer back to Canada for me behind her younger car, and I following in my car. Wasting no time or effort, I placed crystals on the selected mountains as we drove north to Chilliwack, B.C. It was great to be home.

Nari remained there while I drove to Rapid City, South Dakota, and completed a number of grids. Back in Canada I began the task of the lining up the *twenty-one people.* It stands to reason that I would know most of these people, after all one can't just pick names out of the phone book. I made a list of names. When I had the list completed, there were four people in South Dakota, four people in California, including Nari, eight people in British Columbia, including me, and five people in Alberta. That made the twenty-one I needed for the awakening of the Earthkeeper.

While on the plane to Edmonton I connected Northern, B.C., Alberta, The Yukon and Alaskan grids. I was told that the light in the Crystal Grid was now strong enough to extend around the world, and so it was. This grid has Rose-Silver Light, Blue Light and Yellow Light incorporated into it.

Mt. Aylmer, Alberta, **Yellow***; Mt. Robson, British Columbia,* **Blue***; Mt. Olympia, Washington,* **Silver-Rose***; and San Felipe, Mexico,* **Yellow***.*

We have completed 14 grids, seven crystals to a grid for a total of 98 mountains in our section of the Crystal Grid.

I put in this invocation:

All energy or messages forthcoming
Through any crystal I have been given,
Or will give, to anyone,
Will be of the Christed Energies.
No exceptions allowed.
For the Crystal Grid on/in the mountains:
All triangles on all mountains
Are now enclosed in circles,
Bringing in the final step

In the transformation of the planet, Earth.

During the next two weeks there was much assimilation of energies and of the knowledge I received. The job of preparing the information I needed to explain the unexplainable, to twenty-one people, that took a great deal of my time.   Then came the trip to Alberta, and the telephone calls, but eventually I had the permission of twenty-one people. I was given the loan of a string of turquoise prayer beads. Counting the beads I found that they numbered twenty-one, the exact number of people I needed. Interesting little development, wasn't it?

I was made aware that, in addition to my other crystals that I had to take with me, was the pewter elephant and the Seed Crystal gifted to me by *Germaine.

She said, "The knowledge was placed in the Earthkeepers by the Ancient Ones. This knowledge can only be released by the use of a *Seed Crystal,* as it is the key to unlocking the computer in the Earthkeeper."

What is a crystal?

A crystal is the most profound article to be found in the Universe. Once formed, it does not change in form or density; it endures forever. It is moved from one planet to another over eons. It contains within its structure the knowledge of the universe. That is to say, the knowledge is there for everyone to read, if they know how. Indeed there are very few people on Earth today with the ability to read crystals or to retrieve the vast knowledge they contain. I believe that is left for Higher Echelon to discern.

However there is much to be learned from a crystal. They emanate knowledge and emotions that is discernible to those who possess Super-conscious or a Universal mind. Such is the case with the Earthkeepers.

So it is again that the Earthkeepers are here to remind us of our origins. The one on Kauai is the first to be awakened. Its message will be felt throughout the cosmos. The understanding of this event will be recognized by very few humans, but the result will be felt by all humanity. The **WILL of GOD** is being brought forth this day, and will continue for all time. Be not afraid for **GOD** is all forgiving. **HE** is making **HIS WILL** known in many facets of life on Earth and the results are being felt around the world.

This is a time for rejoicing for man is being redeemed.

The next item on my agenda was preparing to go to Hawaii. I arrived in Honolulu one May 15th, 1994 shortly after midnight. My friends were at the airport to meet me. I settled into my 'home' that I was to care-take for the next six weeks. As to my plans, I had checked the calendar and found that the full moon was on May 24th, so I was sure that I would be going to Kauai on that date. Other than going to Kauai I had no other agenda.

Then I heard: ***May 23, 1994; be at the temple on this 5-5-5 day.***

My trip began having overtones at the airport. As I was going to be in Kauai for just one night, I had taken an overnight bag. This was heavy as it contained *the crystal cluster, the obsidian cube, the window crystal, the green calcite wand, the kyanite, the seed crystal, the turquoise prayer beads, and the pewter elephant.*

A young gentleman, who was walking behind me, kindly took my suitcase and carried it onto the plane and placed it in the overhead rack. Such kindness extended to a stranger.

I sat with two Japanese ladies, who were conversing in Japanese. I commented to the one sitting next to me, that her dress was very pretty. This turned out to be sign language as her English was better than my Japanese, but not by much. Her companion showed me her blouse, which seemed to be from Hawaii. She then reached into her bag and gave me a medallion with a bell attached. (Later Nari told me that it was a harmony bell.) I attached it to my white dress so it was with me when I arrived at the Temple.

The Hindu Temple on Kauai overlooks the Wiamella River. It is above the falls and has a wonderful view of the canyon. There is a new temple in process of being built closer to the falls and the stone for the Temple is being processed in India and shipped over to Kauai. This will be the new home of the Earthkeeper.

I arrived and settled in to the hotel ready for the trip up to the Hindu Temple. When I arrived at the Temple the Earthkeeper was wearing a robe of mauve orchids. It was magnificent on its dais with the five-pointed star on the top.

This was the most auspicious day, the 5-5-5, of the Hindu Calendar year.

Gurudeva gave me permission to perform the ceremony. I gave him the seed crystal and asked it to be placed at the base of the Earthkeeper, the point touching the Earthkeeper. I then spread the crystals that I had with me in a certain pattern; the elephant on the extreme left, the crystal cluster, the window crystal, the calcite, the kyanite, and the obsidian on the dais in a semi-circle.

Earthkeeper:
The list of names will be read aloud.
These are the members of the descendants of Ugota
Who have been chosen to be presented to you
On this day, May 23, 1994.
(The names are read aloud and placed on the dais.)
These twenty-one prayer beads represent each of these people
And are humbly presented to you.
(The prayer beads are placed on the list of names in

the shape of a heart)
We ask that you awaken.
That you release your vast knowledge
To the Universal Mind
And to the Cosmos.
This is an auspicious day,
For all mankind and the Universe.

Having completed the ceremony, I meditated and then sat observing the Temple. The crystals remained in position until closing time at twelve noon. I explained that I wished the Seed Crystal to be left in place and that I would be back on the following day. I asked Gurudeva's permission to take a picture. He said this was permissible, but to please wait until just before closing, at which time he'd close the curtain behind the Earthkeeper. Behind the Earthkeeper is a sculpture of Shiva, which could not be photographed.

Shortly before twelve Gurudeva indicated that I should take my artifacts except for the Seed Crystal when I left. I checked in at the hotel in Koloa, and spent the rest of the day sightseeing

That evening I was told that I would be given the next invocation for the Earthkeeper in the morning.

The next morning I drove back to the temple. The flowers had been removed from the Earthkeeper. Reversing the order of the crystals on the dais, I placed the obsidian on the far left, the kyanite, the window crystal, the calcite, the crystal cluster and the pewter elephant.

When I competed this, I noticed I had placed the elephant with its trunk leading away from the Earthkeeper.

These are the members of the descendants of Ugota
Who have been chosen to be presented
To you on this day, May 24, 1994.

(The names are read aloud)
These prayer beads, numbering twenty-one,
Represent each of these people and
Are humbly presented to you.
(The prayer beads are placed on the list of names in the shape of a heart)
All powerful crystal, we ask that you fill
These crystals with your essence
That they may be taken to your likeness and be known.
Your song is being heard.
We will facilitate the awakening of your likeness
As soon as it if feasible.
Thank you, thank you, thank you.

I remained in the temple until noon. Gurudeva was in meditation with the crystal the entire time. At eleven-fifty-five he allowed me to take pictures. He returned the seed crystal. He gave me a card which has a picture of him and the Earthkeeper in meditation. This card had a picture of the location of the temple in the mountains. He gave me a photograph of the Earthkeeper in its robe of flowers taken by a professional photographer. Gurudeva said the Earthkeeper was in a good mood when the picture was taken.

As I was leaving I asked Gurudeva, "Did the Earthkeeper like the ceremony?"

He turned and looked at the Earthkeeper then turned to me and said with a beautiful smile, "Oh, yes."

And so ends my visit and the ceremony to awaken the Earthkeeper in the Hindu Temple of Kauai.

Lord Adonis said that the **ISIS Crystal** was the opening of the next saga. I have explored the energy that an **ISIS Crystal** emits and it is defined as the **Goddess ISIS** and is a female creative power. She is the healing balm for all, whether incarnated in a female or male body. **ISIS** is the power to help balance the emotions so that the male and female sides of each person can unite. The feminine force nurtures and fulfills the heart.

I asked **Lord Adonis** about the explanation of the **ISIS Crystal**. *"The embodiment of ISIS in crystal form is correct. The shape and size are of no importance. What is important is the Embodiment of the Goddess of nature. The Earthkeeper in Kauai is this Embodiment of ISIS."*

Since Nari and I returned from Hawaii in February, I have been busy. This was not my agenda, but the **Light Masters**. It is hard to describe the energy I have been subjected to. The energy in Hawaii was high enough, but after the Earthkeeper's awakening ceremony, I was lucky to know my own name. I was to remain in these energies until I flew home on June26, 1994.

We have established that the energy emitting from the **ISIS Crystal** is feminine. It is an interesting fact that Gurudeva had engineered the delivery of a feminine energy into an all-male Hindu community. The Earthkeeper has been connected to the Crystal Grid and this energy now permeates the grid. I found it intriguing that Gurudeva chose Almitra to find the right Earthkeeper, which was the embodiment of the **Goddess ISIS**. And I, a woman, was chosen to awaken it. Interesting isn't it, being that the Hindu Temple is a monastery for men only.

I have been asked to place an energy circle around the Earth. This seemed impossible to me, being a mere human, but **Lord Adonis** gave me the power to perform this awesome task. This energy started with the Earthkeeper and connected to the following sacred sites: Mt. Haleakala, Maui; Ayers Rock, Australia; Weiser's Stone in England; Atlantis Crystal, Saragossa Sea; Salmon Arm, B.C., Canada;

Dorothy's altar, Chilliwack, B.C. Canada; Mt Shasta, California; and back to Hawaii.

Ayers Rock, Australia: emits the energy of Divine Love.

The Weiser Stone, England: led me to Avalon. Avalon brings transformation and love in a time of confusion and chaos. It is time to unleash her feminine power to bring love into the world, a world ready for change.

The Atlantis Crystal, Sargasso Sea: The Earthkeepers were placed according to the stars and grown by the same technology as the large crystal of Atlantis.

The Atlantis Crystal was not destroyed in the massive destruction, but disappeared beneath the water. The Earthkeepers are to be aligned with the stars again. They will act as antennas for the incoming information to raise the consciousness of the planet. They will be activated in five years, if things go as projected at this time. This will be in 1999.

<u>Dorothy's Altar, Chilliwack, B.C., Canada:</u> holds all the traveling crystal, and the **ISIS Energies**, used in the Earthkeeper ceremony at the Hindu Temple.

<u>Salmon Arm, B.C. Canada:</u> There is a crystal in a lake around Salmon Arm. I have no information other than that.

<u>Mt. Shasta, California, USA:</u> Mount Shasta is the Control Mountain for the Crystal Grid and contains the **OM Crystal** in its base.

I flew back to Oahu, Hawaii to finish the house-sitting job before leaving for home.

This is how the energy was started for the Crystal Grid. Once activated, it has a path to follow as it continues to grow and expand. As other Earthkeepers are awakened in perfect timing, as well as other sacred spots that are being recognized, the energy expands. The more people draw on this energy for their personal growth in consciousness, the stronger the energy in the Grid becomes.

On Sunday, June 26, 1994, I arrived in Vancouver, B.C. Canada. I got the message that I needed to go on retreat to the mountains for three or four days. In my meditation I received this explanation: *"This retreat is for the assimilation of energies, as well as meeting The Masters. We would appreciate you getting a crystal to hold the excess energies in your travel crystals before you go on retreat. It is important to relieve the stress on you and your crystals. Any high place will be fine as long as it's over 2000 feet and quiet. We don't want a place that has been used by other spiritual groups. We neither want to confront their energy or have anyone come in contact with these high energies that we bring. If it is feasible we would like you to arrange this as soon as possible as it will further your development and we can proceed.*

The crystal I purchased was an amethyst crystal which was almost devoid of color, but it is very pretty. I received the invocation for the amethyst:

**This crystal will store and hold all excess energy
From the Earthkeeper "ISIS" until
It is required by the traveling crystals
Used in the ceremony at the Hindu Temple.**

The energy is now sealed in this amethyst and along with the celinite, will help define and magnify the energies that Dorothy has.

Well, a retreat sounded just fine to me as I was very tired. I drove to Manning Park, which is 4000 feet in elevation, and stayed there from June 30th through July 3rd.

Once I got settled in to my cabin I was instructed to place my crystal ball in the center of the bed and to place the single terminated seed crystal with the tip pointed to the heart of the crystal ball and leave it there for 45 minutes. This invocation was given then:

**You are to do as we have directed.
Your work is to begin now.**
(I was told to repeat the above procedure and leave the crystals in place for another 30 minutes. This was repeated three times then I was to take up the crystal ball in my hands.)
**You, (the crystal ball), are to blend your essence
With Dorothy's and no other. This is your task and this
Seals your essence with Dorothy's.**

The large crystal cluster is to be connected to **"ISIS"** now and to Mt. Shasta and the **OM Crystal**. I did that in a simple ceremony. I also connected the crystal cluster to the Lightening Rod, which is a single terminated seed crystal, to empower it for future work.

The large crystal cluster is now connected to **"ISIS"** and has a job to do, I am told. In the absence of another activated Earthkeeper, it is to resonate *like* the **Earthkeeper ISIS**. The crystal cluster is to fill the energy space that is required at this time. When it is returned to my Altar in Chilliwack, it will resonate and be amplified by the agates and the marble. The tourmaline, Spirit Mind and Body, will keep the vibrations on a Christed level. No negative energy will be allowed on this channel. It is sacred to the Light Masters.

The single terminated seed crystal and
The Lightening Rod, holds the essence of
"Isis" and I now seal its energy until needed.
It is to remain in a dormant state and

Cannot be activated by anyone accept Dorothy
(This invocation was given to each of the travel crystals.)
The crystal cluster has now come of age.
It is the backbone of the altar.
Let it be known that this crystal
Acts in the service of God.
It is the keeper of the Master Channel.

I knew that something had happened to me while I was in Hawaii, but I didn't have any way to describe the sensation, my mind felt…muddled and buzzed with all the energy I had taken on. After I completed the invocations on July 2nd there in Manning Park and sealed the energies into the crystals, I went for a long walk, had supper, watched a show on television and went to bed.

Mission completed and what a relief!

I awoke sometime during the night and found I could think calmly again. It was like a large weight had been lifted off my head. I believe that weight was caused by the amount of energy I had been carrying. This gave me an idea of how powerful these energies were.

August 1994
Manning Park

Nari: Dorothy returned to Chilliwack and we settled down in her house. We had several weeks of R&R, a lovely time of just being, going leisurely about our day without any sense of rush or '*have to do*.' We wondered from time to time, if it was over, the heavy push of forming our part of the Crystal Grid since we hadn't heard from **Lord Adonis.**

The funny part of our R&R was that it seemed almost unnatural as we had been in full force since Dorothy laid the first crystal on Mt. Picati in Mexico. Well, maybe Dorothy had more of that full force thing than I did, whatever, it was just different for both of us. Maybe **He** was taking a good look at the physical wear and tear on his human Light Servers.

Well, it was a nice time, but Dorothy or I weren't really surprised when we got the next communication. It was strangely a relief for both of us to know our work wasn't over yet. Perhaps we were getting addicted to all the activity and the excitement of being a part of a tremendous important event. Whatever the reason we were ready as August had rolled around.

One morning **Lord Adonis** communicated with me and told me to go back to Manning Park and bring the Earth Elementals into awareness of the changes that were in the process of happening. This communication explained the need to do this. He said:

Elementals and How They Relate to Humanity

It is sometimes difficult to explain or convince people about the vital importance of natural world and to keep in balance with it, especially with those Natural Elementals that exist on Planet Earth. After all, these Elementals are unseen and invisible to the human eye, yet these Elementals do exist. Anyone who works with plants, instinctively understands, whether consciously or unconsciously, that the health of the plant is due directly to the Elemental or plant spirit in charge of its health and the health of the land. The lands health is the responsibility of humanity in cooperation and in direct connection to Nature. This is why all humans should cherish the land and do it no harm. Your human lives depend upon this.

Humans live in this natural world, under Nature's Laws, therefore are subject to the powers of Nature. Your bodies are made up of Earth's elements that will go back into the Earth upon your physical deaths. It is imperative that humans cease dividing themselves from Nature and seek the balance necessary for the Earth and human survival.

While We help to change human consciousness, We're also impacting the animal kingdoms, as well as affecting the Earth's Elementals and Nature itself.

When We change one thing, We change everything.

Therefore it's imperative that Dorothy and Nari prepare the Earth's Elementals for the changes and the ongoing evolution of human consciousness that will directly affect their well-being.

Lord Adonis

Well, this was our next directive and ours to do. Dorothy selected those crystals and artifacts necessary for the ceremony and we left the next day driving east to Manning Park, B.C. to perform the vital link aligning the Elementals with the Crystal Grid.

Arriving at Manning Park, we and rented a nice bungalow. The crystals that Dorothy was instructed to bring have meanings important to the actual ceremony. It disturbed me that while we were helping to build the Crystal Grid to assist humanity to raise its consciousness and we were here to involve the Elementals in the changes, we hadn't received any directive for including the Animal Kingdom.

I had no idea when I bought the pewter elephant that Dorothy would need it to help activate the Kauai Earthkeeper. Now she told me that this little elephant would also represent the Animal Kingdom in the invocation to come. That greatly relieved my mind.

After setting up the altar as directed, the actual ceremony would include these elements; Fire, Air, Water, Light, Food, Seed of Life, Earth, Pain, Joy, Time, World, Pollutants, Health, Money. These fourteen basic elements are the bases of life on the planet now.

Take out Time, take out Money, take out Pain, and take out the Pollutants and you have the world of tomorrow.

Well, it was an empowering event to be a participant and witness the energy that occurred as Dorothy and I preformed the complex ceremony for the Elementals and the Animal Kingdom that took several days of dedication and prayer.

May all creatures be fully aware
And awake in MY Consciousness
For the world. Let Spirit quicken
The days when we will all be aware
And awake to God's Plan on Earth.

We finished and took another day just to walk the hills and absorb the peacefulness of Nature before returning to Chilliwack. I continued to write and Dorothy had quite a few visitors. Work on the Crystal Grid was at a standstill for the next month. Lordy, we were glad.

It was almost October and time for me to return to the States when I got an invitation to attend a 'Women of Vision' Conference to be held at Georgetown University in Washington D.C. My friend **J**, wanted to go and so did Dorothy, all for different reasons, but it was an occasion not to be missed by any of us. I believe it was the first international conference for women. Certainly it was a stride forward in recognition of the contribution women were making in the world.

Because our friend **J** wanted to go to Washington D.C. She also wanted to attend Torkum Saraydarian's Seminar in Sedona, Arizona on the last of October. She and I decided to drive to Phoenix and tour as many state parks on the way down. We drove down to Sandpoint, Idaho to visit my mother then on down through Idaho, Utah enjoying the beauty of the land. We arrived in Phoenix and left the car at the airport and flew to Washington D.C. Dorothy was to leave from Vancouver, B.C. and join up with us in Washington D.C. And so we did.

Personally, though I was born in Vermont and lived for years close to Boston, MA during the war years, (that's 1940-1945 to the younger readers) my parents had never taken the family to see our capitol. **J** and Dorothy hadn't seen Washington D.C. either, so during the conference, we girls did a lot of sight-seeing and enjoyed it very much. We especially loved the Smithsonian and I got shivers at the Lincoln Memorial; awed at the profound wisdom of this past president, a man who had to have been a **Light Master**.

I enjoyed much of the conference and met some fascinating women, real movers and shakers in the woman's movement. I enjoyed attending lectures with Dorothy and **J** and got a lot out of them. I found it to be a unique experience and one I wouldn't have missed for the world. All in all I was glad I came and I think **J** and Dorothy were too.

Dorothy: I was told before starting on this journey that there would be an Altar in the Convention Room at the University. I was to take my large crystal cluster and place it on the Altar. The Altar was right where I had envisioned it. The crystal remained in place for the entire conference. It became obvious that one of the main reasons I was at this conference was to bring in the **ISIS Energy**. Many of the women attending the conference mentioned to me the effect of the energy from the crystal. I had some very interesting conversations.

I discovered a contingent of native women from the mid-west that were in attendance. They gave me an Indian Prayer Stick. At the time the gift seemed insignificant but later it would be vitally needed in the work that I had to do. I realized I was being used as an instrument to bring this **ISIS Energy** to the women of the world and to the Universe. The crystals belong to everyone and to the Universe. We have them for as long as they are useful to us. When that period is complete the crystals move on.

I enjoyed my stay and in particular, going to Arlington Cemetery and seeing the Eternal Flame on the site of John F. Kennedy's memorial.

Nari: **J** and I flew back to Phoenix and from there we drove up to Sedona to attend the Ageless Wisdom Seminar by my spiritual teacher, Torkum Saraydarian, an Ageless Wisdom Master, who was an international author with more than sixty books to his name. It was, as usual, a wonderful, uplifting time and one of great learning.

After the seminar, **J** and I drove back to Chilliwack. At the border the Canadian Border Agent informed me that I had outstayed my time allotment. They were kind enough to let me get to Chilliwack, pack and load up my car. Twenty four hours later Dorothy and I were heading to California. She was adamant that I not drive home alone, God bless her heart and so off to California we went.

My daughter, Eddi, was ill and needed me to help care for her and the children. Dorothy didn't stay in California long. I drove her to LAX and put her on a plane for home. Wow, what a year! Burning energy left and right! Both Dorothy and I needed some down-time, but would we get it was the question.

After several weeks my daughter got better. Then I fell ill with double pneumonia and had to go to the hospital for a week's stay. The doctor was sure I would die as it was the nasty kind of pneumonia. If it hadn't been for all the Reiki Masters of mine and Dorothy's sending me healing energies I might have done so. The doctor was certainly surprised to see me alive the next day. Ha, fooled him! However, I questioned that dire end as the **Lord Adonis** wasn't willing to let me escape so easily. I still had a great deal of purpose yet to fill. **Lord Adonis** literally had saved my life four times before so I think He helped me again.

STEP 3

Introduction

There comes a time in the evolution of the human race when certain events take place to shock the race into escalating their progress. All these events take place at different times, leading humanity on an upward path. Anytime the human race takes strides forward, there will be a counter active force that will battle to keep things as they are. Only through perseverance will the upliftment of the human race become the new paradigm.

It takes great endurance, patience and determination for those who are striving forward to hold the paradigm in place. Now we are entering into a new dimension. The changing of the DNA is crucial to the physical bodies of humanity in order to keep pace with the spirit, and bring into being the whole human form. It has been the focus of all the Advanced Light Masters, past and present, to assist this major breakthrough. Many have sacrificed themselves in service to this great cause. Many more will do so, but all these lives are blessed for their service, and their reward is greater consciousness.

The DNA work that Dorothy and Nari have accomplished, with the aid of other co-workers, has made a tremendous impact upon human DNA. It is now a fact that the Human DNA is changing.

Many of these life changing events are earth shattering, because they break old patterns and programming's held as holy. We, the Light Masters are here to oversee these turnings and the Crystal Grid has facilitated humanity's entrance into the new dimension; the Fifth Dimension for many, many millions of people.

Read now how this beginning event began to shape humanity's course. Believe that the New Heaven and New Earth approaches with great speed.

Be of good cheer for the events to come will prove the intention of the Many Light Masters work.
Be blessed

Lord Adonis

This is One of the Biggest Event in The History of Mankind

This is How it Transpired.

Multitudes of people have worked on this project. Dorothy Ra Ma Seddon was able to transport this "ISIS" Energy by way of the Crystal Grid to assist the pure female and the pure male energies of the DNA to come into existence.
Apr. 22, 2011:

Dorothy Ra Ma: On being asked to participate in bringing this book into fruition, I have dreaded this part of the work. Being asked to awaken the Earthkeeper on Kauai was one thing, but setting up Altars for the DNA was quite another thing entirely.

I had the time, so that wasn't a problem. In the beginning I had no idea what was going to be entailed or I would have said, "NO WAY". However this is what I had agreed to do before I was born, or so I had been told. Looking back, and as I type this, I know I am going to have to face those powerful energies again. Although this work was done in 1995, and sixteen years have passed since then, the world has not changed enough to support the energies that are contained in this process, so I am going to soften them as much as possible.

And so it is time to relate what happened. It all began with this transmission from the **Lord Adonis**.

Jan.19, 1995:

"The time is at hand for the emergence of the Mineral Kingdom. The part you are to play is of the utmost importance, for unlocking this wisdom is The Stepping Stone for humanity. Your adherence to instructions is of vital importance. The way will be made available to you in the coming months. Your path is preordained. The next step is imminent and cannot be postponed. The stabilization of the Earth's mantle must be attended to, or vast destruction will occur, which is not in accordance with the Plan. Please be aware and be free to travel.

"The coming of age of any society is fraught with problems, not the least is the importance of understanding the universal law of Cause and Effect. WE are going to attempt to alleviate this by giving some insight into the complexities of energy.

"When energy is released, from whatever source, it has a life of its own, and a purpose to fill and a path to follow. When the energy is given a path and a purpose, the energy is disbursed over a wide field of time and space.

"The energies from the Cosmos carry with them knowledge of other worlds, other planets and other beings. Likewise the energy released from these planets carries with it the knowledge accumulated here on planet Earth. All knowledge is ONE. As this Earth comes of age, the knowledge locked within the Earth is being released to the Cosmos.

"This knowledge is of the utmost importance, for it contains the Secret of the Atoms: The Beginning of Life: The Rise and Fall of Civilizations: This knowledge

is ready to be released NOW, as man and the world, are about to evolve into a new dimension, the Fifth Dimension.

"Crystals were used to preserve this knowledge. Crystals are grown in the bowels of the Earth, but the Giant Crystals known as Earthkeepers were brought here at the beginning of this planets life. These crystals, the EARTHKEEPERS, have long since dissolved back to their original atomic form, but the knowledge implanted in the original crystals has been passed down through the ages to succeeding crystals. This is the knowledge, in part, of materialization and dematerialization.

"We are not taking over your life, but We are guiding you in answer to your request to do "GOD'S WILL, and to do your part of the PLAN." There is a vast difference, so be aware.

"It is now time to unravel the secrets of the UNIVERSE so that this Planet and Humanity can move on to do greater things. Millions of years have been spent in achieving what We now have. As there is a purpose to everything, there must be a purpose for Humanity in the Grand Scheme of Things.

"The beginning of this development started with the awakening of "ISIS". In order for this development to continue, other large crystals need to be awakened and connected to "ISIS" so that a grid may be established.

"Earthkeepers will be activated around the globe eventually, making a grid of energy which will benefit all mankind and the universe. This grid will come to pass in the fullness of time. The technology of the use of crystals is in the future or should we say 'in the past to be re-discovered? Know that for this new paradigm to come into being there is much work to be done. One person alone can make a difference. Then how much better

when there is a concerted effort by the many. WE wish that WE could dedicate this work, but that is impossible as this work must be done in the physical world by people. In order for the new regime to become reality, there must be right thinking and right action by the multitudes of people praying for change in the world today to bring this about.

"This energy has brought about a new order in the thinking of the Hierarchy. (The Hierarchy is a governing body of **Enlightened Masters** *working under the direction of the* **LORD CHRIST***) It is making it possible for a peaceful shift to The Aquarian Age. This work must be continued. We cannot tell you what a change has occurred from the reading of the Celestine Prophesies. People everywhere are now contributing to the shift. As this ground swell grows, anything and everything is possible.*

"You must understand that energy is what you live on. All types of energy influence mankind and the planet. At this time, or millennium, in the evolution of the planet, there are energies affecting this world that have not been available for 250,000 years. This energy must have receptors to be fully utilized.

"These large crystals, The Earthkeepers were placed on Earth, at the beginning of life on the planet, as receptacles of knowledge. They were used by the original inhabitants to remind them of their origins. So it is again. As this sun comes closer to the orbit of these planets, vast shifts are inevitable.

"The Crystal Grid that Nari and Dorothy have put in place has given untold benefits to the planet. Humanity gets the side benefits, so to speak. The small crystals that have been connected to the crystal cluster of

Dorothy's, which contains the **ISIS** Energy, *are helping to distribute this energy.*

"The Crystal Grid of Earthkeepers is the next step in the evolution of the planet. When this energy is felt by multitudes of humanity, the real benefits will start to manifest. This energy transcends race, color and creed. There are no boundaries. The energy will encircle the globe and be felt by all people everywhere. They may not be aware of the energy, but they will receive its benefits. **Lord Adonis**

It is important that the readers understand that Nari and I have been working directly under the aegis of **Lord Adonis** and the four **Light Masters** accompanying Him. It wasn't until later we discovered that He was a part of a group of **Advanced Spiritual Beings** that designed, planned, and brought into completion the Crystal Grid and the other necessary works to support the changes necessary for humanity to progress in consciousness.

My friend **T** asked me to set up an Altar for her at Cultus Lake, B.C. not far from Chilliwack where I live. When **T** asked me to do this, she told me that she was working on bringing in the female aspect of the DNA and needed a special Altar. Well that was fine with me. I am only working with the forming of the Crystal Grid. The DNA had nothing to do with me. How wrong could I be?

Among the artifacts I was instructed to take from my Altar was my large crystal cluster, which contained the **ISIS Energies**. I was also to take the seed crystal, the Nativity Figures and my picture of the **ISIS Earthkeeper** to facilitate the setting up of the Altar at her residence.

Please note that I had bought the Nativity Figures in Mexico at the beginning of our adventure. I did not know these figures would be used to set up DNA Altars. Here again is a coincident that was necessary to the ongoing work.

When the Altar was completed, special invocations were pronounced and the room was sealed. We were instructed to leave it that way until the following Monday. I was finished, but I was instructed by Lord Adonis to take a picture of the opening of the Altar.

After I had set up the Rainbow Altar for **T**, I was surprised to be given the information by the **Light Masters** that I would be setting up another Altar. These Altars were to be set up in Canada, because the people who were to bring in the female and the male DNA were Canadians and so was I. Therefore it was logical that the construction of these Altars would be in our country. These Altars were essential in order to energize and empower the Etheric Changes in the human DNA. This was to be the beginning of the DNA work I would be doing. I was shocked indeed by this information. What in the world did I know about human DNA?

I was informed that the reason I was involved in this vital work was to bring about the balance between the male and female energy, like uniting two sides of the same coin. **The Goddess ISIS** *was returning to Earth to bring the female energy into this balance.*

The Altar at Cultus Lake was completed and the energy began to build. It was then obvious to me that the forming of another Altar was necessary to bring in the male DNA. Where this Altar was going to be I didn't know. I understood it was vital that the collective consciousness of humanity would gradually take on the energy of change into their physical DNA without harm. This change in the physical human DNA would then affect the human's mental and emotional bodies, thus bringing about their evolvement into the Fifth Dimension.

(Everything happens first in the etheric body of any living species, as well as the Earth, before physically manifesting.)

I was instructed to go to Medicine Hat, Alberta where I was to set up a vortex. Medicine Hat is 722 miles from my home in Chilliwack, B.C., with a driving time of 12 hours. Yes, Canada is a very BIG country. I'm not too sure why I had to successfully open this vortex. I had no idea how this vortex related to the work I was doing on the DNA, but I faithfully followed my guidance. I simply was told to go to Medicine Hat where I would receive further instructions.

Talk about going in blind! Well, I hadn't seen my family in Medicine Hat for a while, so this was a good excuse for a visit.

The complexity of actually opening up a vortex is not a simple thing to do. Number one, you're dealing with Earth Energies; two: you're dealing with **Light Masters** approval and; three: the 'how to do it.' Since I had the approval of the **Light Masters**, it was a matter of communicating with the specific place where the vortex was to be opened. Not an easy thing to accomplish and it took me some time. I searched and discovered the perfect place that wouldn't disturb people. I actually *felt* the approval of the Earth and Its permission to open up a vortex there. That surprised me, but it encouraged me into the next step that was the 'how to do it.'

I began to gather certain articles that would facilitate me in doing this. They were four pewter thimbles, five pieces of petrified wood, Ostrich Feathers, a map of Alberta and cigarette ash. Well I had everything except the cigarette ask. Now I was almost ready. It all turned out to be simple. I asked my niece, Rosanne, if she would give me her cigarette ash, which she did. Behold, the vortex opened! *I felt it open!* How strange is that? But it was exactly what happened, and don't ask me how or why.

While I stayed with my family I received the next instruction. I was to draw a triangle on the map of Alberta. Since I already had the articles that I used to open the vortex, I only needed a crystal. However I still didn't know where I was to go in Northern Alberta. Alberta Province is *huge* and extends far north to the Northwest Territories which border on the Arctic Ocean. I had no idea *where* exactly I was to construct this second Altar and I needed a point of reference before I could draw that triangle.

I called Nari and she said for me to contact her friend in South Dakota where I'd find my answer. Well, we chatted a while and I asked her how she was feeling. Poor Nari was just recovering from double pneumonia and had been hospitalized for some time. It amazed me how many healers are troubled with ill health, at one time or another. However Nari was recovering and we sat up a regular Sunday contact for our conversations. Though we were separate, we remained in necessary close connection as the work went on. Nari was always there to answer questions, give me moral support, or to channel for me. Thank **GOD**, for it made it easier for me to continue on.

Well sure enough her friend gave me the name of **W** who lived in a town in Northern Alberta. I contacted **W** and she invited me to her Wholistic Health Center. Now I could draw the triangle.

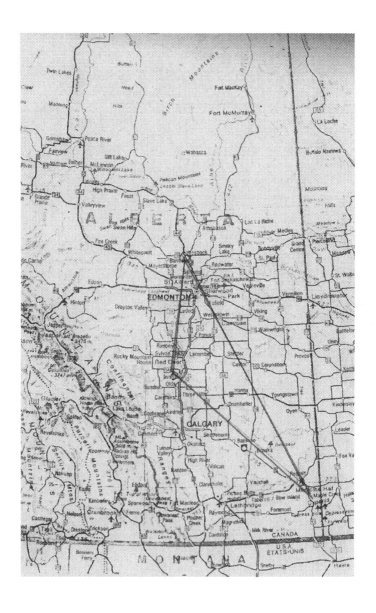

This triangle connected Innisfail to the Town, where **W** lived in Northern Alberta, and to Medicine Hat. Then I drew a forgiveness symbol in the center of the Triangle. I placed a thimble, a piece of petrified wood and one of my crystals at each point. The figurine of Mary was placed at the Town in Northern Alberta, and the baby Jesus was placed at Innisfail, while Joseph was placed at Medicine Hat.

It was at this time that I became aware that there were other triangles to be drawn. I questioned this and received a yes and a description of the drawing. It was to connect the Altar, which I was to build in Northern Alberta, to the vortex at Medicine Hat, the Cultus Lake Rainbow Altar, and interestingly enough to Innisfail. It made for a very interesting picture.

The Nativity Figures are once again in the picture. I can only conjecture that it was necessary to connect Medicine Hat with Northern Alberta and to Innisfail, as it is my birth place. It has been written that we are connected to the Earth at the place where we were born. So my being connected to the Earth at Innisfail might be the reason for the triangle, which was important to the ongoing work.

I have come to realize that this work, which I thought was separate from me, is in fact a part of me. It dawned on me when the triangle was formed it connected me to the Earth.

I was led to open a vortex at Cultus Lake, British Columbia, where I had long ago purchased a summer cottage, and spent a lot of time there when my children were growing up. It seemed to link me again, with this new endeavor.

It was later revealed to me by **Lord Adonis** that I was an *Earth Master,* just as Nariananda was termed a *Sky Master.* Well, that certainly clarified the whole mystery of my easy dealings with the Earth. I also realized that I could not do the work without growth. The work cannot proceed without my growing apace and keeping up with the advancing knowledge and energy. I must adjust on all levels. It is my understanding, or lack of understanding, that sets the pace of the work.

Interestingly enough, I had begun clearing my etheric bodies back to the DNA prior to this new work. I saw the subtle changes in my family after I had done this clearing. Was this all part of the plan too? Apparently! At the time I didn't see the connection, and it was only later that I got this overview.

Six hours and 430 miles later I arrived at **W** center and met her group. As we were setting up the Altar I was introduced to **R**, who told me he was to bring in the male DNA and needed help energy-wise to complete his part of the plan. I established the Altar and placed the various articles, including the Indian Prayer Stick I received at "The Women's Conference" on its shelves with my crystal cluster that carried the **ISIS Energy** on the top shelf. Again, **Lord Adonis** wanted me to take a picture of this Altar.

At this point I got a clear picture of a completed drawing of the DNA. I immediately sat down and began to draw it. I got a 'spiritual slap' across my head and a, **"No, not yet."** Did I stop? You want to believe I did. Obviously this drawing was before its time. Then I got another picture, one that was much, much more simplified. I drew it. Yet, I got the strangest feeling that this picture was the first of many. Why these pictures had to be slowly evolved, I didn't really know for sure, but it appeared to have special significant importance to the procedure. Well, I am obedient if nothing else.

I also was given to understand that it would take some time to increase the energy to the point when it could be utilized. To do the work and not know the reason why, can be very frustrating, but I was afraid that if I pushed too hard for the *'why'* I might screw up the work.

The drive home from Northern Alberta to Chilliwack took me 11 hours and 656 miles. Needless to say by the time I got there I was fairly exhausted.

I questioned the reason for the complexity of the articles I had to gather and why they varied. I was told that each Altar was different, so different articles were necessary in order to move the energies around, thus building their power. Even though I didn't completely understand, I was proud to serve without question, as I was sure that at some future time I would be given full understanding.

I was resting at home when I had a sudden revelation as to why the pewter elephant that Nari had given me was vital to the awakening of the Kauai Earthkeeper, and why it was necessary for it to be included in the articles I was to take when energizing these two Altars. Pewter is a symbol of protection. Elephants symbol success, so the pewter elephant looked after both of these requirements.

I had a further revelation, one that shocked me. *I was connected* to the **ISIS Energies!** That's why my physical presence was needed to carry them back to Northern Alberta and empower the Altar. After I had done that, and the energies of both Altars had increased in power until the **Advanced Masters** could take that power and begin the Etheric Changes in the Human DNA. The energies in the two Altars were building; I could feel them.

Well, this was a definite surprise, however as I prepared to take another road trip. I need to tell you how difficult it was to carry these powerful **ISIS Energies**. If people could only experience them, then they would believe how hard it is on the whole body. Nevertheless, I would do it. I asked my grandson to take the trip with me and help me carry these energies so that I could drive. He agreed without questioning me why this was necessary.

Before going north, we stopped at the Cultus Lake Altar mainly to make contact with it and **anchor** the **ISIS Energy** there. Before leaving I took another picture of the Rainbow Altar.

We left immediately and took the northeast route that was fairly direct to the north-country through Jasper Pass into Alberta and proceeded to the Town where **W** lived.

After we arrived, **W** and I put a new bookcase in the Altar room and put all the various elements I had purchased on the shelves, which were a few stones and specific crystals.

I was instructed to place my large crystal cluster, holding the **ISIS Energy,** and the seed crystal on the Altar touching the new Quartz crystal. These crystals were to remain on the Altar until Thursday.

There were seven of us that helped **anchor** the **ISIS Energy**. After this was completed, I took my crystal cluster off the Altar for its presence was no longer necessary as the Quartz Crystal was now a substitute.

I would like to add here **a** general dedication/invocation, one that would cover the basic intention for forming these Altars in the first place. Mainly because there were numerous specific invocations used, which would be boring for the reader to wade through, but needless to say, they were all *vitally* important to the actual work, but not necessary to repeat in this accounting.

The Energies of these Two Altars are connected.
The Rainbow Altar at Cultus Lake and the Altar in Northern Alberta.
These Altars are now activated and are
Joined together in the name of the Christ, to serve
The New Order, the New World and the New Dimension
Of human consciousness.
These Energies are sealed in Divine White Light.
They are to be used for advancing Humanity as a whole.
They are connected to the Crystal Grid.

Before leaving **W** asked me if I would address her group. I was at first hesitant to do so, but decided that people needed to have a greater understanding of what was being done.

We gathered in the great room and I will admit to being nervous about talking to such a large group of people, as this wasn't a normal thing for me to do. However, as I stood before them I felt overcome with peace and I knew exactly what I was going to say.

"Good evening ladies and gentlemen. My name is Dorothy Seddon and I work for the *Hierarchy* headed by the **LORD CHRIST**. My personal guide is **Lord Adonis**. I wish to explain a bit about the energies that we are putting in place here. As you know energy is neutral so we must be careful that the energy that we are receiving is from Divine Origin. This is why we have put the Guardians of the energy on the Altar. This energy is for your evolvement and it is to help you in your realization of the reality of *who you are*.

"The Altar is not to be worshiped, but it must be honored and respected. As you grow in your individual paths, you will find the energy will challenge you. Sometimes you will hate it as it will bring up things that you don't want to see. But remember, you can't have growth without change. You can't reach your full potential if you are carrying a lot of garbage, either from this lifetime, or from a past life. You are all here at this time to experience this energy and to grow from its presence.

"It is important that you receive direction from your guides. If it doesn't feel right, ask, "Is this information of the Christed Energy?" This is one of the cautions we give light workers. Because of your light, you will attract negative energies. The dark forces cannot live without Light so therefore you, being of the Light, they will be attracted to you. If you make this inquiry, "Are you of the Light?" Then, *whoever they are*, must reply truthfully. You simply say, "In the name of CHRIST be gone!"

"Much of the work we do often boggles the minds of people, yet **LORD JESUS** said, "**Greater things shall ye do that this.**" **HE** was speaking of HIS miracles. In bringing in this vortex and energizing the Altar here we are simply doing one of those *'Greater things.'*

"One of the hardest lessons I had to learn was not to doubt. To accept the fact that indeed; *I can do these greater things and so can you!*

"Thank you for listening. **GOD** bless you all."

My grandson and I were to leave **W's** town in Northern Alberta, and drive south to Medicine Hat the next day. I was given to understand that I was to make the loop south to Medicine Hat, and from there head west along the border of Canada and the United States, thus carrying the **ISIS Energy** both ways in a somewhat elliptical circle back to Chilliwack.. That was understandable since we had taken the northern route up to Northern Alberta and now were looping back west. Our southern route going west was going to be interrupted because the Crow's Nest Pass over the Cascade Mountains on the Canada side was under construction. So we dropped down into the States and drove west through Logan Pass, Montana.

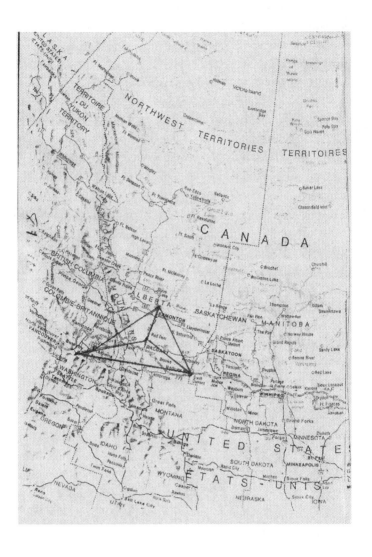

This was where we experienced car trouble. I guess nothing ever runs as smoothly as expected. Just as we passed the lodge, at the very peak of the pass, the engine failed. Suddenly we were without power, no steering and no brakes. We began to speed down the other side of the pass, a very *steep, winding* road. I managed to quickly pull off the road into a bank where we were abruptly stopped. Better to damage the car slightly then have a run-a-way down the other side of the pass. You can imagine my grandson and I were scared to death at our near miss. We sat in the car for the next twenty minutes just thinking about it. *It suddenly dawned on me that our Guardian Angels were still keeping an eye on us. Thank you Guardians!*

It seemed to be a long time just sitting and wondering what we were going to do next when I decided to turn on the key. I was very surprised when the engine fired. Driving carefully on, we entered Canada through the Idaho border crossing. I was tempted to kiss the ground by the time I reached home. I didn't, of course, but it was a near thing.

I learned later, when I took my car to be checked, that the cause of the near accident at Logan's Pass was an overheated fuel pump. I was lucky to have been able to drive all the way home; another miracle? I believe so. Of course the fuel pump was immediately replaced.

I didn't have too much leisure time before the next call upon my services. I have an acquaintance whose name is **JJ**. She called me and asked me if I would build her an Altar on Promontory Hill. She implied that she thought that her Altar would better spread the energy, being up on a high hill, than the Altar at Cultus Lake. I saw no harm in this. However I first checked it out with **Lord Adonis** and He said:

The importance of this Altar is to spread the Isis Energy throughout this province. The Cultus Lake Altar

is coming down. To build this Altar on Promontory Hill is imperative to anchoring the triangles and retain their empowerment.
Lord Adonis

JJ and I built the Altar. I took my crystal cluster with the **ISIS Energy** and the seed crystal and placed them on the Altar. **JJ** brought her articles and when the Altar was completed I was given to give this Invocation:

The energies started here today will continue for all time.
These energies, as part of the Elohim Altar, will bring in
The necessary energies to insure that this project
Called "The Enlightened City," will be a complete success.

My mind was boggled. What was this about an Enlightened City? Chilliwack? Well I knew that this city began with total prohibition and possessed 21 churches, but an enlightened city? I don't think so.

Lord Adonis said, **"There is a Golden City hovering over this whole region."**

What? We're under an Etheric Golden City?

Well, that might explain what we're doing here. In a way it is just something more to think about. Is it a possibility? Maybe, I'll leave this up to the readers.

Given this new information I asked if the Cultus Lake Altar cancelled out the vortex there? I was given to understand that the vortex is very much active and that it is now connected to the Promontory Hill Altar.

I continued to draw the DNA pictures as they were passed down to me. Finally, in September, I received the last drawing. As I drew this last picture I realized that, even though this was a completion of sorts. The information was being dispersed into the collective Crystal Grid. I sensed that I still had work to do with the DNA. Now what would that be? It was a mystery so far.

Ah, the revelation! I was to put the formula for the DNA changes into the crown chakra of anyone who wanted it. It surprised me how many people volunteered which kept me busy for some time.

I was meditating one morning when I perceived that the Altars I had built in Cultus Lake and in North Alberta had shut down. I must say I panicked a bit thinking I had done something wrong. I immediately contacted **Lord Adonis** and asked if that was true. His reply was:

Yes, quite true. Once the Altars energies had reached maximum, the Light Masters took the energies to empower the changes they were making in the Etheric DNA. The reason behind these simplified drawings of the DNA, which you have been doing, has been to send these changes down into the physical through these drawings; one change at a time in order to soften the final change in the Human Physical DNA. When you received the final drawing, it was placed in the Crystal Grid. When that happened, Beloved, all Drawings of the DNA and all information as to how this occurred are to be sealed and not revealed at any time unless the Light Masters permit it. No further information on the DNA work will be given. Good work.
Lord Adonis

> **Evolution:**
> 20,000 years ago, the splitting of the DNA, Atlantis.
> 10,000 years ago, Confucius brought in <u>Wisdom.</u>
> 5,000 years ago, Lord Buddha brought in <u>Light.</u>
> 2,000 years ago, Jesus brought in <u>Love.</u>

The amalgamation of the Male/Female God Force will bring in the <u>Power.</u>

We have the Male God Essence in the cells of humanity. October will see the emergence of the Female God Essence in the cells of humanity.

If humanity is going to evolve we must have access to the full blown DNA. Nari and I are not the only ones that put crystals on/in the mountains. This is a world-wide phenomenon. These world-wide grids have access to the female energies through the Circle of Light that was formed around the world.

The sections of the Crystal Grid were brought under the umbrella of Mount Shasta in December 2001. It took seven years for this to be achieved but in the grand scheme of things, this is very quick indeed.

We have always known that we had two strands of DNA. The other ten strands were dormant until re-awakened in 1995. We haven't had access to the other 10 strands since Atlantian Days.

I can tell you that the DNA changes were reported by doctors in 2002.

I Quote:

"October 26, 2002-Patricia Resch reported the geneticists were finding that the DNA was changing." This report was just seven years after we completed the Etheric DNA work.

"September 20, 2008: Extracted from an article "The Bigger Picture" by Susanna Thorpe-Clark in "DNA and Body Changes and Remedies." She quotes the article by Patrica Resch.

What do the 10 strands of DNA mean? This is the crucial step to the Fifth Dimension.

October 4, 1995: Each person has 2 strands of DNA, 10 strands of Latent DNA and two strands of God strands of DNA. These two God Strands are invisible. When the work is complete fourteen strands will be operating. They will have been triggered into existence.

When the Female God Energies are put in place, it will trigger this latent energy and it will be as though it has always been. The sequence for this happening was vital. Had one portion been triggered ahead of the others, the physical body could not have been able to withstand the strain of the change.

It was necessary to have a period of time between each happening to give the physical body time to adjust. The integration of all this will take a year.

Prophecy by Brian Grattan:

Brian Grattan wrote an article in the wonderful magazine called *"Sedona Journal of Emergence."*

Quote: He said that there is a spiritually accelerated window of sorts on the Earth from the year 1988. (This is the anchoring of the Mahatma Energy, to the year 2028.) During this forty year period of spiritual acceleration on this planet, we would accomplish more spiritual growth than in the previous 3.2 billion years of our Cosmic Day." Unquote.

Explanation as reported in "The Complete Ascension Manual" by Joshua David Stone:

Quote: A Cosmic Day lasts 4.3 billion years, so we have 1.1 billion years left in the Cosmic Day of our section of ***GOD'S INFINITE UNIVERSE.***

Just think about that! In this forty year span of time, we will make more progress than we have made in the past 2.3 billion years. It is an amazing time to incarnate on the planet. Unquote.

(For further information on the changes in human DNA in this year of 2011, please Google: Changes in the DNA. Many websites will be listed for your additional information.)

Dorothy: In conclusion, the work on the DNA was finished. It took six months to bring this to finalization. Oh, what a relief! Now maybe I can rest and get back to normal living. The work is done.

As I explained at the beginning of Step 3, I was not looking forward to revisiting the energies of the DNA work. It was actually worse than what I had anticipated. The difference in the energies in 2011 as compared to the energies of 1995 is enormous. Researching and writing about the DNA is like having one foot in yesteryear and one foot in tomorrow, or one foot in the Third Dimension and one foot in the Fifth Dimension.

The question: Was it all worth-while? The answer is a resounding YES. The Crystal Grid was designed for humanity. Is it working? YES!

When you look at what is happening in the world today, what with the middle-east in an uproar and several other countries following their lead for change in the way they are governed, people are changing. They are demanding democracy and freedom.

Canada has just had a general election. The results were astounding. The leading Liberals, who have been around ever since I can remember, were ousted. The official government is now the Conservatives. Most of the old guard were defeated or retired.

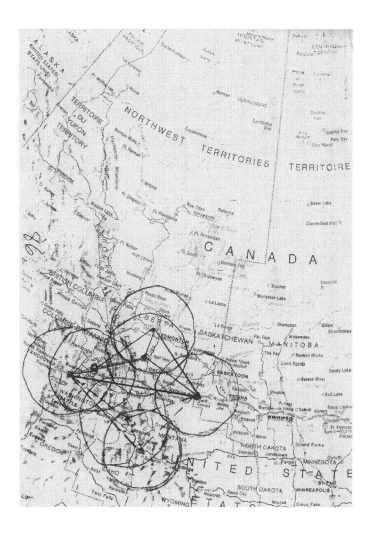

Here are the final two maps which completes the work I was instructed to do.

Change is in the air and that is a good thing. Is this due to the Crystal Grid and the changes in the DNA? In my opinion, YES!

And so ends my work for the Light Masters in changing the human DNA. I have been blessed to have served them. I thank Nari for being the voice of **Lord Adonis** when I needed clarification, and thank her for her support though this difficult time.

Dorothy Ra Ma Seddon

STEP 4

Introduction

Now comes the time for the additional processes that will accelerate the evolvement of human consciousness. Once these processes are given to people who want them, and these processes and the people's experience of them are put into the Crystal Grid, they will begin to affect humanity as a whole.

The purpose of these processes that we are giving Dorothy is to introduce changes into the physical, emotional, and physical bodies. Thus it has been accomplished and thus establishing a form of etheric guidance for other people to follow. The power of these processes to change the responses to the coming changes, are phenomenal. Needless to say the leading edge is being made by the people who courageously volunteered to partake of these advanced processes.

To prepare them for the ultimate duty of helping bring the grids that had been developed around the Earth into One Crystal Grid.

Next on the agenda are the ceremonies to be performed for the 7-7-7, the 8-8-8, 9-9-9, the 10-10-10 and soon the 11-11-11. We gave Nari powerful symbols representing each of the last three cycles to empower these ceremonies. The 12-12-12 will be fore coming in the future.

The work continues and as it does the Crystal Grid grows in strength, and in power and it is influencing the consciousness of the people around the world.

Behold! The coming of the New Age, the Aquarian Age is here!

Lord Adonis

Duties Divides Temporarily

Nari: I left Canada for California in October of 1994 to take care of my daughter, who was ill, and her family. In the following weeks, she got better and was able to go back to work and attend her family. I had my own plans as to what I was going to do next, when I came down with double-pneumonia that put me in the hospital for a week. My doctor told me I was very seriously ill. The man kept repeating that as though to prepare me for death, as if I couldn't feel it creeping in.

I called Dorothy and had her call all our Reiki Masters to send me Reiki healing energy that night. I called my Mother to say goodbye in case I did pass over. If I hadn't done so, my Mother would have somehow come after me. (She was a very strong psychic so I believed her. Besides, she would never forgive me if I hadn't called.) Of course she wanted to fly down immediately, but I talked her out of that because, if worse came to worst, and I died in the night, she would be too late. I said for her not to be afraid as I knew where I was going if I died, so just say a prayer and if I was still here in the morning I'd call her right away. She wasn't at all happy, but Mother was powerful in prayer so I wasn't especially worried.

Was I afraid to die? No, I prayed that I would live, if I hadn't finished serving my purpose, but other than that, I just gave my spirit over to **WILL OF GOD**.

I had to laugh at the look on the doctor's face in the morning to find me alive. Such is the power of prayer and Reiki Healing Energy. I guess I had over twenty-five Reiki Masters sending healing energy to me through the night. So obviously I was alive which meant I hadn't completed my purpose. Again, I believe that **Lord Adonis** stepped in once again, and saved my life, as he had done four times before. After all, He had taken years to train me and that would be such a waste if I was to die before finishing what I had come to do. You can imagine I didn't mind at all!

Perhaps I need to explain the healing modality of Reiki according to **Him**. The explanation of the reason **He** wanted me to be initiated into Reiki back in 1986, shortly after **He** contacted me to act as **His** channel. At the time, Reiki was the most powerful healing energy on the planet, and also the Healing Light of Reiki opened a persons' spiritual center, the Third Eye, and awakened the Seat of the Soul. It would make **His** ability to channel through me easier if my Crown Chakra was open.

So now I think people need to know more about how Reiki would affect our future work that had to be based on a group of Reiki Masters.

"*It appears that this is the time to explain Our need to base future activities upon the necessity for all participants to be Reiki Masters. Reiki raised the vibrations of a person many times higher than persons without Reiki. This raising of vibrations was essential to the work We demanded of them. Also they needed to be spiritually awakened. That happens when the Third Eye is opened, a spiritual center that allows for visualization and the expansion of one's consciousness. The opening of the Crown chakra to the power of Light awakens the Seat of the Soul, the Pineal gland that's found in the exact center of the skull. The future, vital*

work requires that these Reiki Masters be in a state of highly advanced vibrations and ready to combine with the powerful processes that We would be giving Dorothy in the future."
Lord Adonis

Most of 1995 was taken up with healing as I went back to the hospital a few more times. Yet gradually I grew in strength at last. Dorothy was very busy with her new purpose which was working on the Etheric DNA. It was all most mysterious to me, but she was under the direction of the **Light Masters** and I channeled **Lord Adonis** for her when she needed more direct answers.

Dorothy: A message came to me that I was needed in Las Vegas. My daughter and I flew down to Nevada with my 'traveling crystals,' the same ones I used in awakening the **ISIS Earthkeeper** in Kauai. The next day I was guided to drive out and visit as many churches as possible. With my traveling crystals in the trunk of the car, I managed to *touch* many churches in the six hours of driving before returning to the hotel. The next day I drove for two more hours and got in touch with a number of other churches. On the following day we drove out into the country to enjoy the peace and silence of the desert.

That night I asked why did I have to touch all these churches?

It wasn't long before I got an answer. ***The churches break the illusions of the city. Connected together, these churches represent a spiritual force and are sources of goodness.***

Immediately a vision of a huge triangle connecting Las Vegas to the triangles formed in Canada. I had to draw it and record that for the future.

We returned to Canada soon after this revelation, and it felt good having served another mission successfully.

After the hectic pace of 1995 bringing in the DNA, my life returned to normal, whatever that was. I was kept busy teaching Reiki in the ensuing years and that made me happy with life, doing everyday chores and taking occasional trips. I initiated at least forty Reiki Masters. These people became my friends. We worked together to clear off negative influences that we had created in this ongoing life, as well as our past lives.

Nari: My Mother came down to live with me from Sandpoint, Idaho in 1996. We bought a double-wide mobile home in Huntington Beach, California, just a few blocks from where my daughter lived. Dorothy and I kept our Sunday talk schedule throughout these intervening years, so we never lost contact, but kept each other in the loop.

My mother was diagnosed with terminal cancer in 1998. She was told she had three months to live. This was devastating news to both of us.

My Mom calmly said, "Well dear, I guess **GOD** has remembered me after all."

She was 93 years old and sharp as a tack. We enjoyed each other's company and got along amazingly well. Such courage to face the final months, and I could only applauded her, while silently grieving at the coming loss of a much loved parent, but also a dear, dear friend.

I had been caretaking her 24-7 for the past 2 months, and I was becoming very tired. Dorothy called me on a Sunday as usual and propose to come down for a visit if it could be arranged, and take me away for a few days. I knew that the final month of my mother's disease would be extremely grievous and stressful, even though my daughter would take that month off to help me so I could get some rest. I called my sister, Joan, in San Antonio, Texas and asked her if she would come over and spell me for a few days. She flew in right after Dorothy arrived in Huntington Beach, California. Dorothy and I took off for Las Vegas. That's when she told me we were on another mission. That was okay with me, I was enjoying just being free for a while. Caretaking is tough job, if you're doing it right.

We arrived in Las Vegas in the high, dry heat of the dessert. It's always a shock to the system to adjust from the cool, humid beach weather to high, hot, and dry dessert country. We drove up to Mt. Charles, as it was apparently necessary to get into a higher in altitude, as well as to get out of the dense negativity of Las Vegas. There, under the guidance of **Lord Adonis,** we performed a sacred ceremony.

Dorothy was directed to cut all control lines, from other planets, to the governments in control on Earth. Thus the people of the world would be set free over the course of time and would liberate themselves mentally, emotionally and physical from the negative influences of their governments and advance into the new age of higher consciousness.

We returned to Huntington Beach within a few days and Dorothy left for home. My mother entered the final month of her life. It was the hardest thing I've ever had to face was to watch her die a little more each day. One feels so very helpless to stop death. I talked to her constantly even though she was comatose, for people hear even though they are unconscious. She died in October of 1998. Shortly thereafter I went to Canada to visit Dorothy and recuperate from months of caregiving and to grieve for my loss.

Dorothy: In May of 1999 I put the Reiki symbols into the Crystal Grid to add to the ongoing raise in human consciousness.

In June of 2000 I was instructed to buy the Bio Genesis material. I was very reluctant to buy this as the price was astronomical. I agreed only after it was pointed out to me that our next step was to heal with color and sound. I took delivery of this product in Payson, Arizona. I was given a couple of brochures which I have long since lost. Checking on the internet in March of 2011, I gleaned this information.

In 1997 Cindy Kroeger (her maiden name) had a visit from a Celestial Being. He introduced himself as **Lantos**, an **Ascended Master.** This was the advent of the BioGenesis Tools.

In February of 1999 he gave Cindy detailed instructions on how to build a "Geneses" device, a pyramid-shaped device which a Harvard-trained mathematician later verified, was designed precisely with the same proportions of the Great Pyramid of Giza. **Master Lantos** said this device would be used to energize various materials, such as glass, which would be used to give Light and healing to the people.

Master Lantos approved and even redesigned the glass pieces Cindy obtained from a German glassmaker, and told her the purpose of each piece and how **He** wanted each piece named and 'trained' in the **Genesis Device.**

Master Lantos: *"BioGenesis is the Birth of Creation. We instill the remembrance of the Process of Creation into a glass, and that glass radiates, or re-educates, its environment with the memory of the process of Creation. Restoring the memory of this Process within an individual or object creates a living system—it becomes living matter."*

While this ancient technology has not been on Earth since the days of Atlantis, **Ascended Masters** recently re-introduced this effective energy to the world.

As you can tell from the dates, I ordered my material soon after the **BioGenesis** was put on the market. The Bio Oscillator supports the removal of toxins from persons, animals and the environment, removes negativity stored up over centuries within people, and supports the removal of infection from the body.

I wanted it, but unfortunately, it was not available for another few months. They only had a few in the expected first shipment, but one was reserved for me.

From the BioGenesis Brochure: "This precious technology has been handed down from Atlantian days and before. It has been tens of thousands of years since this technology has been functioning on Earth. The Earth rejoices at the return of the Light of BioGenesis."

In the year 2001 **Lord Adonis,** as channeled by Nari, gave me the first process, one of the thirteen processes that were to follow. These processes were designed to raise human consciousness. A nucleus of people volunteered to be initiated into these powerful processes, thereby strengthening their own development on all levels of consciousness. As these people accepted a process it was automatically placed in the Crystal Grid for the benefit of humanity.

Lord Adonis: *"These processes respond differently to each individual. Dorothy disclaims any responsibility for the results experienced. These processes are always done with the intent for the highest and best good for each person and with harm to none, and where necessary, under the preview of the Karmic Lords."*

(This was one of the first assignments given to me that included the use of BioGenesis)

Earlier in June of 2001, I came down to visit Nari. We drove down to San Diego, California. We visited a large bookstore looking for something to read. As I walked down an aisle a book suddenly fell on my head. I picked it up and read, "The Seven Mighty Elohim Speak." I figured that spirit wanted me to read it, so I bought it.

Nari: the funny thing about this kind of thing, books that, seeming well secured on the shelf, will suddenly 'fall' on you. I've had similar happenings and the books were always timely in their arrival. Spirit's taking a helpful hand? Yes, I believe so.)

Dorothy: Let me explain who the Mighty Elohim are:

"The Seven Elohim are mighty Beings of Love and Light Who responded to the invitation of the Sun of this System and offered to help to manifest the Divine Idea for this System, created in the minds and hearts of our Beloved Helios and Vesta-God and Goddess of our physical Sun Itself.....Call to these Great Elohim in all the sincerity of your hearts! Daily invoke Their light and understanding to come into your own consciousness!.......As you have been told, the Seven Rays of the Seven Mighty Elohim are anchored in the forehead of every physical form and, through the expansion of these, We are able to reach into your worlds to help you, if you will allow Us so to

do. Of course, We never intrude in any way, for your God-given gift and prerogative of the use of your own free-will is always paramount! You see, from the beginning, it was intended that the Elohim, Archangels, Chohans of the Rays and Angelic Hosts were to be a constant daily association with mankind, as They are on Venus and other planets; and have been, all through the ages. However, the "veil of maya" (effluvia of discord) gradually became so very thick around the planet Earth and the actual bodies of the people that WE could not get through to their consciousness at all. I think there has never been a recorded time on this planet when the Elohim and Archangels have spoken to the people of Earth in consecutive order as has been done here recently. I believe the Chohans have."

I believe this gives people a clear understanding of the help that is available to us from the spirit world if we ask for it. Well, the book set me on fire and I did invoke their light and understanding to come into my consciousness.

I was shock to be contacted by **Them** with a message that I was to go to Salt Spring Island, British Columbia, Canada, which is in the Strait of Georgia, between Victoria and Vancouver. I and five other Reiki Masters were to visit a Reiki Master that had a summer home there. (All these Reiki Masters had been initiated by me.)   I was directed to perform a ceremony with the help of these six Reiki Masters, and the use of the BioGenesis wheels and tools. I was given the words to invoke the Ceremony:

We seven, representing the Seven Mighty Elohim,
Do hereby declare the rejuvenating energies of
The Great Planes of this continent of America
are hereby Activated, Harnessed and Directed
to The Crystal Grid, Anchoring on Mount Olympia.
I hereby ask the Reiki Masters located in the local areas
to anchor the energies directed from

Salt Spring Island, B.C., Canada, to Mount Laguna,
San Diego, California, Superstition Mountains,
And Camelback Mountain, Arizona,
South Dakota and Mount Robson, B.C.
We seven Reiki Masters representing
the Seven Mighty Elohim
do hereby declare the energy now
anchored in the Crystal Grid and grounded
at Mount Olympia Washington,
is hereby directed to be spread over the Desert,
Plains, Mountains, Lakes and Rivers to enhance
all living things in the areas they so lovingly guard.

It was a joy to us all to have served **The Mighty Elohim** and we were honored by representing them on planet Earth.

We all had a great time and enjoyed the island accompanied by our mascot, the Crow. Now let me tell you about the significance of Crow at our island retreat.

The following quote is from the book, **"Medicine Cards"** by Sams and Carson. These are wonderful cards and the explanations are equally insightful and artistically done.

Quote: "Since Crow is the keeper of sacred law, Crow can bend the laws of the physical universe and "shape shift." This ability is rare and unique. Few adepts exist in today's world, and fewer still have mastered Crow's art of shape shifting. The art includes doubling, or being in two places at one time *consciously:* taking on another physical form, and becoming the "fly on the wall" to observe what is happening far away.

Human law is not the same as Sacred Law. More so than any other medicine, Crow sees that the physical world and even the spiritual world, as humanity interprets them, are an illusion. There are billions of worlds. There's infinitude of creatures and Great Spirit is within all. If an individual obeys Crow's perfect laws as given by the Creator, then at death he or she dies a Good Medicine death—going on to the next incarnation with a clear memory of his or her past.

Crow is an omen of change. Crow lives in the void and has no sense of time. The Ancient Chiefs tell us that Crow sees simultaneously the three fates—past, present and future. Crow merges light and darkness, seeing both inner and outer reality." Unquote.

I found that Crow figured very strongly in representing the Animal Kingdom, the Physical World and the Spiritual world, and in the end, it's all really ONE.

Dec. 17, 2001:

Dorothy: Since Salt Springs my life calmed down somewhat again and by the time December rolled around I was preparing for Christmas, when **Lord Adonis** gave me this process that included all the other **Light Masters** and Their grids that had been formed around the world. Using the power of BioGenesis, I was to do this process once a week for the following five weeks. This took energy and concentration and for whatever reason this process had to be done for such a long period of time was never explained to me. I was just to do it. This is the intention **Lord Adonis** gave me.

"This intent is to connect all of the Crystal Grids on Planet Earth.
All who are involved in forming Crystal Grids on the Mountains of Mother Earth will now release their grids to the
Control Mountain of Mount Shasta, California, U.S.A.
Under the direction of Dorothy, Ka Ra Am Ra,
For the Highest and Best Good of the Planet."

Nari: In 2002 I left California in the fall to visit my sister, Joan, and her husband in San Antonio, Texas. It had been a few years since I had seen my Texas family. It was also a great time for me to finalize the publishing of my book, 'Echo of a Dream.' I enjoyed nine months with them, the longest time I had ever gotten to really know my other family.

In May of 2003 I left San Antonio for Denver, Colorado, where I stayed with a friend and found a job as Assistant Manager of a high-end retail store. Later in that year, Joan called me and told me she was dying of cancer. I immediately got time off for a few days and flew to Texas to see her. Sadly, I had to go back to Denver, leaving her to leave this world without my presence. A few weeks later her husband, Roy, called me and told me Joan had died. I grieved for she was a much loved sister. I think it was **GOD'S** special blessing that called me to visit Joan for those nine months and to have those precious memories of our laughter and companionship, which proved so valuable to me after her loss.

Jan. 20, 2002

Dorothy: As part of the ongoing process dealing with the combining of the Grids, this was the next step. The control mountain for this sector, Mt. Olympia, will now carry this intent to Mount Shasta. This was the Intention.

> *"All mountains now connected to Mount Shasta will have an*
> *Amplifier placed next to the crystal now in place.*
> *These Amplifiers will be as large as necessary,*
> *And will face east and the rising Sun.*

Lord Adonis and The Light Masters.

From the time I purchased the BioGenesis tools and wheels in the year 2000 I was given a total of fifty-seven processes. In turn they were to be given to my Reiki

Masters. This was a very gradual process that would increase the frequencies of everyone without stressing anyone. When I asked them about the results, I received this answer: They felt wonderful but very subtle.

My daughter Maggie, her children were grown and on their own, so she sold her home and moved in with me. This made a lot of sense, as both of us were living alone. In 2004 I decided that I had had enough of climbing stairs as the home we had was a three level town house. While I was in Arizona visiting friends, my children, Jim and Maggie, found the perfect place for us to renovate and move into. This fourth floor, two-bedroom apartment has a wonderful view of the mountains surrounding Chilliwack. This apartment complex is very much in demand as it is handy to the Chilliwack Mall.

Nari: In June of 2004, I quit my job in Denver and made the decision to go full time as a writer. I was just turning 69 years old, and if I didn't follow my heart's desire then, I'd die with many regrets of 'would've, should've and could've.' No thank you. I would rather strive hard to be a successful writer/author. And even if I failed in my attempt, I would have felt good about having given the quest my 'ALL.' I was free for the rest of the summer and spent it visiting friends and family. I drove over to Blaine, Washington to visit my sons, meaning to stay for the holidays then go south to California. It never happened. I became ill and was to live in Blaine until I got better. **Lord Adonis** had other plans for me. But I was glad to be only 45 minutes away from Dorothy and Maggie when tragedy struck their family.

October of 2004:

Dorothy: Maggie's son, Joshua, lost his life in a car accident. If that wasn't grievous enough, her brother, Jim, my son, passed away in his sleep in March of 2005. Joshua was 24 years old and Jim was 54, both too young to die. This was a time of unbearable grief for Maggie and me, one that took a long time to heal. Maggie's other son, Dustin, makes his home in Chilliwack, as does Jim's daughter, Monique. That closeness helped and was a comfort.

Nari and I and Maggie had suffered grievous losses in a short two years. We understood each other's grief, but Life has to gone on. Emptier for the loss of loved ones, but we know life is to be lived the best way we can manage. So Nari and I both bore the pain and grief of losing beloved members of family.

After four years of using the BioGenesis Tools and Wheels they have become a part of me. They no longer feel abrasive. These tools contain the most powerful energies on the planet today. To adjust my energies to these tools took some doing. I intuitively sensed that they contain Fifth Dimensional Energies.

Lord Adonis explained to me that **Master Lantos** had put governance on the BioGenesis Tools. I can see why that would be necessary. The only way to bypass these governances was for me to work with the tools and wheels until I could raise my own energies to match theirs.

One day, after I had adjusted to the energies of the BioGenesis tools, **Lord Adonis** declared:
"Dorothy is a Master of BioGenesis Energies."

So that was Nari's and my life as we settled down for the next few years. Meanwhile, I concentrated on doing the processes that would raise the frequencies of my Reiki Masters.

Nov.1, 2005

Nari and I were directed to go to the Las Vegas where we had some work to do at the Luxor Pyramid Hotel.

Nari: Now I had always disliked the energies that were emitted by the black pyramid of the Luxor Hotel and Casino. I had never gone there during the many times I visited Las Vegas. To be told we had to perform a ceremony there crept me out! Well, ours was to do and endure the creeps, I guess.

Dorothy and I arrived and walked into the Luxor. We were to go in as far as we could to be as close to the peak of the pyramid as possible. Interesting enough we found a very nice spot that had a beam of light shining down on the floor not too far from where we judged was the center. The Luxor was crowded with people, yet there wasn't anyone around us at the moment, as we stood in this center of light coming, perhaps from a sky light, or so I believed. Maybe it was something else entirely.

Dorothy: We assisted **Lord Adonis** in putting a BEAM OF LIGHT from the Luxor Hotel to the center of Mother Earth. We held, in our hands, my Cathedral Crystal, my Seed Crystal and the BioGenesis Translator.

In addition to the Luxor, six gateways were put in place. These gateways consisted of a Light Beam going to the Center of the Earth to stabilize the West Coast of the United States and Canada. In all, we placed seven beams of Light; two in Nevada, four in California, and one in Washington State.

Nov.2 2005 **Luxor Hotel, Los Vegas, Nevada.**
Nov.9, 2005 **Sacred Gardens, Los Angeles, California.**
Nov.10, 2005 **Mount Shasta, California.**

From Dorothy's living room in Chilliwack, B.C., we placed a beam of light on Mt. Baker.

Dec. 8, 2005, **Mount Baker, Washington.**
In the following year Nari and I flew to California to place the remaining beams of light.
Feb.7, 2006, **Mount Tam, San Francisco, California.**
Feb. 8, 2006, **San Francisco Cathedral, California.**

I asked **Lord Adonis** for an explanation.
"This work has made the West Coast of the continent safe. California is not going to fall into the sea."

July 24, 2006:

Dorothy: I received a phone call from Helen, a Shaman as well as a Reiki Master. She said she wanted to come visit us if we were going to be at home. Of course, she was welcome as she was also a good friend. Unknown to all of us, **Lord Adonis** was going to use the three of us, Helen, Nari and myself to pull in a primal energy from the universe which we were to send to Mount Cheam at Chilliwack, B.C. When we had completed this task Adonis instructed us in how to energize other quartz crystals with this energy.
Dictation By **Lord Adonis:**

Universal Crystals:
It is our intention that this Universal Power
That has been formed by the Universe and Mother Earth
Shall be used in a Continuous Flow
To the Crystal Grid Surrounding the Earth.
The energy includes Love, Peace, Beauty,
Harmony, Balance, Compassion, and Abundance.
Raising the Spiritual Consciousness and God's Will.
The Increased Energies will bring about
God's Plan on Earth.

In 2007: **Lord Adonis** gave me this advanced process, as channeled by Nari, to promote the clearing of negative memory patterns from the Etheric Body, the Astral/Emotional Body and the Physical body.

This process clears the three permanent atoms, the Physical, the Astral/Emotional and the Mental Permanent Atom. These atoms are the recorder of our past lives experiences that our spirit/Soul carries from one lifetime to another. Out of these Permanent Atoms our physical, emotional and mental bodies are formed for each life.

Many people feel helpless to break the negative habitual patterns that are so destructive in their lives. This process takes out the incorrect coding in the DNA of inherited negative tendencies. It removes this coding from the Permanent Physical Atom. It removes the residual effects in the physical body. The healing is spread over a period of six months. All addictions, related or unrelated, whether you are aware of them or not, are going to be affected by this process.

I did this process on Nari and myself. I was instructed to do this process on twenty-five people before the **Circle of Light,** to be held on September 9th, 2007, (another 999 day).

This meant that I had seventy-five processes to do in fifty-four days. I had to organize the Circle of Light. Looking back on these instructions I realize this process was similar to the process I was given for strengthening the DNA formula. In doing this repetitive process I was able to strengthen that process in the Crystal Grid.

September 9th, 2007: (9-9-9): Chilliwack, British Columbia, Canada, thirteen people gathered to hold the

Circle of Light. *There were thirteen people, five* **Light Masters**, making a total of 18=9; a **Christed Number.**

The following invocation was put into the Crystal Grid at precisely 11 m, PDT.

The Three-Fold Heart Flame, Pink, Gold, and Blue,
Now enters the Etheric Body of the Earth.
It now enters into the collective Etheric Bodies of Humanity
To clear away all compulsive, addictive, destructive behaviors
That is contra to the evolution of human consciousness.
Under the aegis of the Universal Light Masters and the Masters
Within the world, all the Light workers will be able to receive
Such a blessed healing for those who wish to accept it.
In the name of the Christ, In the name of Love.

November 9th, 2007: The Circle of Light:

Nari: We all gathered in Dorothy's home to perform a ceremony which will be very empowering. Dan represents the Male Energy, Dorothy represents the Female Energy, **Lord Adonis** and the **Four Light Masters** and **Nari,** represent the Androgynous Energies. This made a total of eight.

Lord Adonis explained to us that at precisely 11 Am PST, we would be joined by the **CHRIST ENERGY,** making a total of nine. The **CHRISTED ENERGIES** would be projected into each of 150,000 circles being held at the same time.

November 9th, 2007: This ceremony is to be the reversal of September 11, 2001, we were asked to reverse the shock of the destruction of the World Trade Center in New York City and erase the negative reactions.

In the name of Light and of love and of Power we
welcome
The CHRISTED ENERGIES at the ninth participator,
as HE is in all ceremonies now.
We do the will of the Light Masters of which we are
part.
The combination of Light and Love Energies is now a
pendulum
The insurgence of these Energies are pouring into the
Crystal Grid
And it is now a controlled motion.
The pendulum will continue to swing, bringing in these
energies
On every level, in the name of CHRIST.
We send blessings of Love and Light to all humanity
That through the activity of these energies they will
Change the consciousness and the hearts of humanity to
Accept the New Heaven and the New Earth.
To accept the Christ Consciousness of Love and
All Universal Laws.

The Grace Light was brought to the Planet with the advent of the Full Moon of Cancer. This Light was placed in the Crystal Grid by **Lord Adonis,** Master Dorothy and me. This light will increase your intuition, improve your health and enhance every aspect of your daily life. The more you pull in the Light from the Crystal Grid you will receive the Grace Light Energy, similar to Reiki, but greatly amplified. Master Adonis tells us that many entities have incarnated on this planet, at this time, so that they can take the Grace Light with them.

(**Dorothy Ra ma Seddon: Please note: Now that these processes have been put into the Crystal Grid, I am no longer available to do private sessions. I have retired from active service in this regard.**)

Dorothy: In Preparation for the 999 ceremony I was given to understand that we would need the Quartz Crystal Cluster from my Altar, and the BioGenesis Scepter. Knowing that we would need something to hold the crystal I purchased a TV table, and made reservations at the lodge in Manning Park for the night of October 8th, 2009. We were told to expect visitations when we performed the 999 ceremony. Now that was a surprise. Just who was going to appear?

The ceremony was to be held on the mountain's summit at Manning Park. We explained to the **Masters** that it would be dangerous to do this ceremony at Greenwich Mean Time, as that would be 2 AM PST. Navigation on this mountain road is tricky at the best of time, but in the dark, no way. **Lord Adonis** decreed that the Masters would coordinate the different times into a focused transmission of energy.

THE 9-9-9 CEREMONY:
October 9, 2009, at precisely 9 AM;
Manning Park, British Columbia, Canada
At the Lookout, 5,380 feet above Sea Level
Lord Adonis, Attending Light Masters,
Nariananda and Dorothy stood facing East.
They both held the scepter pointing at the Crystal Cluster.

Lord Adonis Speaks:

"We are gathered here in the presence of the Light Masters and in communication with all other Light Masters and their Light workers around the world. It is agreed the time is now to open the portals in the Crystal Grid and other designated portals.

We, the Light Masters and our Earth Masters do now open and expand the portals in the Crystal Grid and expand the other portals established by our Masters, Nariananda Mayo and Dorothy Seddon. These expansions are to be performed in a graduated manner over the coming year to be ready for the 10-10-10.

The collective energies of The Christed Love Energy are now being drawn into the physical plain, through all the vortexes and portals, into the higher consciousness of humanity. Those whose hearts are open will accelerate and those whose hearts are on the cusp of opening will do so over a graduated time of one year, so as not to shock the mental, emotional and physical bodies.

Thus it is done. Thus all is now activated according to the Lord of Love and the Power of God, so that God's Plan may be restored to Earth, as for-ordained.

We, the Masters on Earth, Mid-World and Heaven, so decreed this to be so, with the blessing of THE CHRIST.

OM, OM, OM

Imagine our surprise and shock when Master Adonis introduced the **GODDESS ISIS.** Nari channeled the **GODDESS** briefly. I didn't understand a word that SHE said through Nari, but I knew from the gestures that SHE was adding Her blessings and Her Energy to the Energies flowing into the Crystal Grid. What an Honor!

Thank you, Thank you, Thank you.

I asked **Lord Adonis** what **THE GODESS ISIS** had said. He explained that in Universal Language, each word holds a multitude of meanings, so a literal translation was not possible. Basically what the **Goddess** was imparting was HER special blessing of Love in all directions on EARTH. That this visitation was to affirm the connection of the importance of the Control Mountain, Mt. Shasta, California, which has the **OM Crystal** buried in its base. From there, the LOVE ENERGY circulates through the Crystal Grid as ordained by the nine **Light Masters** of the **Circle of ONE**. These **Light Masters** have worked for the past millennium to perfect the creation of the Crystal Grid.

Last, but not least, a special blessing was bestowed upon Dorothy from **"ISIS"** for her love and her dedicated work. For being willing to channel **HER** energy, Nari was also receptive of the same blessing.

Thus Lord Adonis interpreted "ISIS" speech, as SHE was the ONE around whom the Circle of Nine Light Masters worked.

Lord **Adonis,** as channeled by Nariananda Mayo:

"The 9-9-9 has activated some very ancient crystalline fields of metamorphic stratum on the earth. These are powerful stratums that emit a crystalline field. The most potent of the Metamorphic Crystals are the Canadian Shield, the Acasta Gneisses in northwestern Canada, the Isua Supracrustal in Greenland, The Lower Shield in Minnesota and Michigan, in ancient crustal rock in Swaziland and in Western Australia. All are connected to the Grid and are activated in sentience and unity into the New Earth."

December 13, 2009:

Dorothy: I had a small stroke. Maggie realized what was happening and promptly sent me to emergency. After many tests and diagnosis, my Doctor put me on blood thinners. After I had been on the blood thinners for a while, I began to feel better.

In July of 2010, I was diagnosed with Hemochromatosis, as if dealing with a small stoke wasn't enough challenge. Hemochromatosis is an overdose of iron in the system. I was sent to the hospital for a phlebotomy (blood-letting), a regime that has taken many sessions to make my system use up the excess iron. This seems to be working.

I want people to understand that, while I am an *Earth Master*, so stated by **Lord Adonis**, I am in this physical body, which is ageing and subject to all the physical ills that can befall any person, I take no pride in saying I will overcome these ills and will continue to persevere in serving **Lord Adonis** and the attending **Advanced Light Masters**. To be born into this world one can expect to encounter difficulties and dis-easement/ills, throughout one's life time. This world is a world of learning, challenges and personal victories in overcoming such hindrances.

I had been told by **Him** that Nari was a *Sky Master*. Well, Nari and I have been opposites in many ways, but we always seem to balance each other which made an interesting balanced whole. Duality made into complements.

I received this email from **Lord Adonis**, as channeled by Nari, late in August.

Beloved Master Dorothy:

As we said when WE last met that WE would be telling you about another purpose you will be serving in Arizona.

The increased universal and world energies, during these present times and in the months following, are escalating the tensions and chaos within that state, which if not cooled, will flow over into the southwestern part of the United States creating great disturbances.

It is by the order of the Circle of ONE that you perform two major events. One: You are to take selected crystals from your Altar and some of the BioGenesis Tool and wheels which will be needed for a ceremony to be performed on the energy cleared land of Eva's home. There is a small metal sculpture on the front lawn that will anchor the intention for the betterment of all concerned. The invocation will be given to you after you arrive in Phoenix.

Two: After this ceremony has been completed, you will then plant the three programed crystals on Camelback Mountain, which will help dampen the fires of chaos around this state. You will choose these crystals before leaving Canada; two quartz crystals and one Obsidian, (black crystallized rock). You will intuitively know which crystals will have the potential to take on the needed Energies.

Marry the first crystal to OUR Crystal Cluster and empower it with Light and Tolerance. Marry the second crystal to the small 'ISIS' Crystal on your altar, for Love and Compassion. Energize the Obsidian with Balance and Calmness. Take these empowered items to that designated mountain. They represent "THE POWER OF THE TRINITY."

Thank you. Blessed be your journey. Call upon us for assistance, if necessary.
LORD ADONIS.

Dorothy: *To marry a crystal, I first cleanse the new crystal of all impressions left on it by previous handlers. Then I transfer*

the energy from the designated crystals from my Altar, by rubbing the crystals together. I put the invocations into the crystals and then seal in these energies and I did the same for the Obsidian.

Before I began packing, I had a very clear vision of a vast dark blanket separating Phoenix from another Etheric Golden City that lay above it. Obviously the purpose for the ceremony and the invocation was to clear this dark energy.

I contacted my friends in Phoenix to tell them when I would be arriving. So in September of 2010, I flew to Phoenix and they met my plane. I explained to them what I had come to do and the importance for ceremony. My friend Eva, one of my Reiki Masters, volunteered to assist me in this.

The next morning, I was meditating when **Lord Adonis** gave me the invocation for the ceremony that I would be performing in Eva's front yard that day. She and I gathered up my tools and went into the yard. There with the aid of the BioGenesis Tools, we performed the vital ceremony.

We command in the name of the Christ that the sense of Of impending doom and chaos be lifted from this state. That the Etheric Golden City poised over Phoenix be Respected, and that the Light Masters are once more Empowered to bring Peace and Tranquility to Phoenix And the surrounding environs.

Often, when performing such dramatic and powerful ceremonies, it is necessary to keep it very quiet. Dark forces taking whatever form is usable and could possibly interrupt this needed ceremony, so I was more or less flying under a blanket of protection. Eva and I felt a great accomplishment having completed the greater part of the mission I had come to serve for the **Light Masters.**

On the same day Eva and I found the perfect place on Camelback Mountain to plant the three crystals, '*The Power of the Trinity',* was what I heard.

Well, my mission was accomplished and the results were the calming of volatile energies in Arizona. I rested and visited with Eva for a few days then flew home. It felt good to have successfully completed my task without any trouble.

October 20, 2010:

10-10-10 Ceremony

Four Triangles
9:30 AM
Represented at this ceremony are:
The Light Masters of the Circle of ONE
Lord Adonis
Nariananda
Ra Ma

It is the will of the Circle of ONE, and THE LORD CHRIST that We open all the vortexes to receive the inflow of the Christed Energy into the Earth.
Following this empowered Love will be the Grace Light that brings WELLNESS into the Earth and into Humanity.
The Duality that has infected great harm between Masculine & Feminine, Man & Nature, Spirit &Science, Soul & Intellect, Physical & Spiritual, and between Light & dark forces, are receiving a very special Energy of dissolvement-thus bringing about a gradual unity of opposites.

Thus is the Will of God, thus it is the Will of the Light Masters on Earth, Mid-World and Heaven.
It is complete

Lord Adonis

(A summary of the cause and effects of the 10-10-10 by **Lord Adonis**)

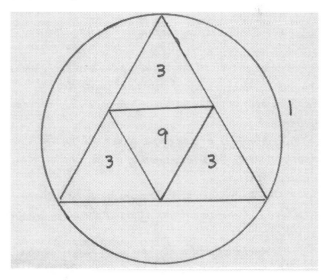

We here-in give you the symbol for the 10-10-10. This symbol is, in essence, the Trinity. The triangles are there to represent the coming together of dualities that signify the joining of energies that have been opposed to each other for far too long.

There are ten energies altogether:

> *The energies of Masculine verses Feminine*
> *The energies of Soul verses Intellect*

The energies of Physical verses the Spiritual
The energies of Spirit verses Science
The energies of Nature verses Man

Under the Christed number of 9, all is being gathered into oneness, hence the Circle represents the ONE; 3+3+3+1=10=1

The Forces are powerful in opposition to this inevitable work,

Yet it will become one in its timely fashion.
The trinity of 3 represents Light, Love, and Power.
It is not in duality with the Father, Son, and Holy Ghost.
The power of the joining of here such triangles
Bring into being the Christ Energy to weld the differences together.
It is the symbol of Christ's appearance on Earth,
The long awaited Messiah, Lord of Light, Love and with the Power of God.

The Multitude of Ceremonies of the Master-led groups around the world has affected the consciousness of humanity

As a whole, and will continue to do its work.

With the expansion of the vortexes in the Crystal Grid, There has been a deeper anchoring into the Earth Physical of increased Light, Love and Wellness.

Wellness is part of the Grace Light and these powerful energies will greatly accelerate the advancement of human consciousness into the Fifth Dimension.

Wellness is also represented in the triangles.
Wellness of mind
Wellness of heart
Wellness of the body physical
With wellness comes peace

Wellness clears the mind, heart, and body of hatred and brings into being goodwill because wellness is a gift of God's Love.

The 10-10-10 furthers the abilities of these Energies To strengthen and help advance man's will to overcome the dark forces.

The United States of America carries the torch, the Light of Freedom.

It is being challenged within and without its borders.

The Light of the Statue of Liberty is symbolic of what people stand for regardless of nationality, religion, or culture.

It is the great driving need in human hearts for freedom that the Light Masters of the World, Mid-world and Heaven seek to support.

You have seen the progression that has brought us all to this pivotal point. You can see the forward development of the on-coming times.

Nothing can stop this upward movement of humanity into the greater expansion of consciousness and into the Fifth Dimension, eventually.

We will be with you prior to the holy ceremony of bring the Christed Energy into the Crystal Grid and into the Planet Earth.

Blessed be thee, good servants of the ONE, blessed be the events that will bring triumph of Love into being. As above, so it is below.

All is one,
All is One,
ALL IS ONE.
Love and Blessings,

Lord Adonis

STEP 5

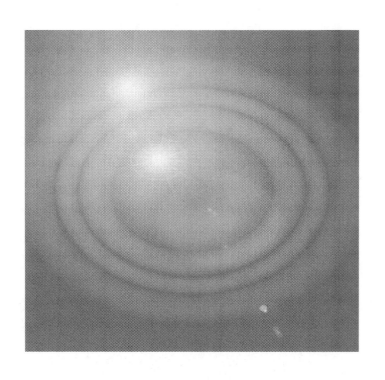

The Unfolding Times

This is the beginning of the new age of reason. We greet you all in the name of Love and Light, as God's Plan is being restored on Earth.

As it is with all great changes, chaos begins the breakdown of the old paradigm of conscious behavior and replaces it with the new paradigm of Peace. The stronger the old programming the more difficult will be in breaking it.

When resistance to this destined changeover is ridged, all negative forces and powerful programmed responses, must be broken, often causing violence.

So Beloved People, you who are of the Light, will and must stand up for Freedom and Peace, which are virtues of the highest ethics.

If We, the Light Masters on Earth, Mid-World and Universe can assist you to help ease this changeover of the way the world thinks, acts and responds to events, We shall answer.

It is seen that sacrifice must be part of the changeover, as the breaking of the old paradigm will not be accepted without fall out.

Indeed, much will be the violence of the times until the dark forces are defeated. When the balance has been struck, then the Light will overcome the dark, then shall Help come from other Universes, from other highly developed planets, where either the dark forces will be absorbed into the Light, or those people who cannot accept the new order on Earth, will be taken to another place, another planet where they can continue learning the lessons that those of you of the Light have already learned. Then there will be peace, goodwill and brotherhood for Humanity.

Just because the way things have always been on Earth; war, conquest, massive destruction of lives, destroying nature and all the other vicissitudes of Life on Earth, doesn't mean that what We have been working for, what We have constructed, offering influences to strengthen the consciousness of humanity, can't be realized.

Again, it is the matter of breaking old habits of thought, breaking the control over lives by the powers that are now controlling world events.

Change one thing and you change everything else. Change threatens peoples' security and that threatens their survival. One person changing their minds from negative to positive action in order to bring about peace in the homes, peace in their community, states, nations, will gradually influence humanity's consciousness. Thus is the power of one person's Light.

It is time for the individual to take responsibility for their very thoughts, words and actions. If there is to be a return to freedom and peace, each person, trying to live in the Light and Love of GOD, regardless of what name the Creator bears, must be willing to enact peace in whatever situation presenting itself.

There is Power in Love; love of Self, love of family and friends, love of country and now, broaden your view of greater love for the Planet Earth and encompassing all people.

And so, Beloved, is the challenge that faces you. We have done what We have been allowed to do without interfering with your free will. Be sure your free will, GOD'S Gift to you, is used well. You will be held accountable for your choices.

The Universal Laws will someday be the rules under which man will live. Such Laws were written many thousands of years ago, to guide, and protect mankind. If you are not aware of such Universal Laws, We recommend that you acquaint yourselves for your further education.

The Law of Cause and Effect is plainly seen in the activities on Earth, as now they are being played out. Violence begets violence; hatred begets hatred, goodwill begets goodwill, love begets love, and so on and so forth.

If the majority of people on Earth desires Peace, which is a Cause, then eventually Peace will be theirs, the Effect.

And so We, the Ascended Masters, Advanced Masters and Universal Lords, serve the Light and the Love and the Power of GOD.

The great conflict is upon you. What the people of the Earth do will be reflected out into the Universes. The Earth is the final testing ground of whether Humanity will survive or destroy itself for all time.

If that should happen, then the Earth, a living Entity, will also die.

We tell you this truth for all people to be made aware, if you aren't already, that the Great Testing is upon you. We believe, My brothers and sisters of the Light, that the turning point has already been reached and that the majority of People of the Earth are dedicated to Love, and Peace. Thus they will triumph over the dark, destructive forces trying to obliterate all life that desires Peace and Goodwill for Humanity.

So be of good cheer, those who work for Peace, those who live for the Light and the Love of all people, *for you will obtain Freedom from chaos and live in the New Heaven and the New Earth.*

Be strong, be brave and face the chaos of the times for this chaos is simply demonstrating the breakdown of ridged belief systems and ridged programming.

You are living in a wonderful and awesome era of change. You were born into this time to bear witness and contribute to this awesome change.

Celebrate this Event, and add your Light and your Love to the growing energies in the Crystal Grid which will empower the People of the Earth to End the Time of Sorrow.

Let the New Paradigm Be! Let the bells of freedom ring once again in every Nation. Let the Universal Laws be the rule for all People and all people will live under THE GREAT CREATOR OF ALL LIFE and UNIVERSES, THE GOD OF MANY NAMES, FOR ALL HUMANITY.

I am LORD ADONIS and with my fellow Light Masters of many degrees, rejoice in our labor to assist Humanity to step into the Fifth Dimension of Consciousness.

There is your goal, there is your destiny. Live toward that day when it shall be as it was meant to be, GOD'S Plan restored on Earth.

We leave Humanity with Our Crystal Grid filled with Power to enact changes for the highest and best good of all People without regard to nationality, culture, race, or religion.

Blessed be all People of Goodwill.

Peace We also bless you with, and so it shall come to pass.

We watch and wait and help when called upon.

LORD ADONIS

Epilogue

This has been a work of love, regardless of the length of service, sacrifice, effort and all the trials and tribulations we humans have to put up with to get anything of value accomplished.

Whether this story of ours is believed or not believed, matters little. We have our experience of serving under an Enlighten Being, **Lord Adonis**.

We are reporting this event in this book form as this is what **Lord Adonis** and the other **Light Masters** desired us to do; inform the people of the world that there are Advanced Beings who are striving with us to bring about changing the world into a Peace Consciousness.

Dorothy and I have both looked back at the past eighteen years and agreed that the effort we've made has been worth the price we have paid. And so it is with our fellow light servers around the world.

These past eighteen years seems to be such a little time to have been involved in this great earth shaking event, The Crystal Grid. Over these past years, we have seen vast changes occurring in world events, the breakdown of governments, the changing of the human DNA, as well as the advancement of human spiritual consciousness, all to bring about the New Heaven and the New Earth.

It is only in looking back can we see the changes that have and are happening so rapidly that it leaves a person bewildered at the speed of time.

So here ends this saga, this tale, of Master Dorothy Ra Ma Seddon and Master Ruby Nariananda Mayo. We release this book to the readers to believe or not to believe the happenings of that time. All we know is that miracles happened in our lives.

Time to let go and let GOD'S PLAN be restored on Earth. We have done our part and will continue to obey the call to serve humanity and the **Lord Adonis**.

GOD Bless all the people of the Earth, and a very special blessing for the Earth itself.

And so it is.

Ruby Nariananda Mayo and Dorothy Ra Ma Seddon

The Great Invocation

*From the point of Light
within the Mind of God
Let Light stream forth into the minds of men.
Let Light descend on Earth.*

*From the point of Love
within the Heart of God
Let Love stream forth into the hearts of men
May Christ return to Earth.*

*From the center where the Will of God is known
Let purpose guide the little wills of men
The Purpose which
the Masters know and serve.*

*From the center which
We call the race of men
Let the plan of Light and Love work out
And may it seal the door where evil dwells.
Let Light and Love and Power restore the Plan on Earth.*

Many religions believe in a World Teacher or Savior. Such names as the Christ, the Lord Matraiya, the Imam Mahdi, the Bodhisattva, the Messiah are used in some Christian, Hindu, Muslim, Buddhist, and Jewish version of the Great Invocation.

The Invocation belongs to humanity, no particular group or organization is sponsored. It is a world prayer with no personal or material urge, such as prayers asking for divine assistance for one's self or loved ones. It expresses humanity's need and pierces through all the difficulties and doubt, straight to the Mind and the Heart of the One in Whom we live and move and have our being-the One Who will stay with us until the end of time itself and until "the last weary pilgrim has found his way home."

Men and women of goodwill throughout the world use this Invocation in their own language. Further information, translations, and copies of the Great Invocation may be found through:

The Lucis Trust
120 Wall Street, 24th Floor
New York, NY 10005 USA
Reprinted with kind permission
www.lucistrust.org

Reference Books Used in Quotes for The Crystal Grid

1. "The Crystal Journey" by Almitra Sunrise Zion 1991
2. "The Compete Ascension Manual" by Dr. Joshua David Stone
3. "Medicine Cards" by Jamie Sams and David Carson
4. "The Seven Mighty Elohim Speak" by Thomas Printz
5. The Crystalline Transmission" by Katrina Raphaell
6. "Earth, The Pleidian Keys to the Living Library" by Barbara Marciniak. No book.
7. "Love is in the Earth" by Melody Pyrite
8. "Echo of a Dream" by Ruby Nari Mayo